1,000,000 Books

are available to read at

www.ForgottenBooks.com

Read online
Download PDF
Purchase in print

ISBN 978-1-332-82555-4
PIBN 10086344

This book is a reproduction of an important historical work. Forgotten Books uses state-of-the-art technology to digitally reconstruct the work, preserving the original format whilst repairing imperfections present in the aged copy. In rare cases, an imperfection in the original, such as a blemish or missing page, may be replicated in our edition. We do, however, repair the vast majority of imperfections successfully; any imperfections that remain are intentionally left to preserve the state of such historical works.

Forgotten Books is a registered trademark of FB &c Ltd.
Copyright © 2018 FB &c Ltd.
FB &c Ltd, Dalton House, 60 Windsor Avenue, London, SW19 2RR.
Company number 08720141. Registered in England and Wales.

For support please visit www.forgottenbooks.com

1 MONTH OF FREE READING

at
www.ForgottenBooks.com

By purchasing this book you are eligible for one month membership to ForgottenBooks.com, giving you unlimited access to our entire collection of over 1,000,000 titles via our web site and mobile apps.

To claim your free month visit:
www.forgottenbooks.com/free86344

* Offer is valid for 45 days from date of purchase. Terms and conditions apply.

English
Français
Deutsche
Italiano
Español
Português

www.forgottenbooks.com

Mythology Photography **Fiction** Fishing Christianity **Art** Cooking Essays Buddhism Freemasonry Medicine **Biology** Music **Ancient Egypt** Evolution Carpentry Physics Dance Geology **Mathematics** Fitness Shakespeare **Folklore** Yoga Marketing **Confidence** Immortality Biographies Poetry **Psychology** Witchcraft Electronics Chemistry History **Law** Accounting **Philosophy** Anthropology Alchemy Drama Quantum Mechanics Atheism Sexual Health **Ancient History Entrepreneurship** Languages Sport Paleontology Needlework Islam **Metaphysics** Investment Archaeology Parenting Statistics Criminology **Motivational**

THE PRIVATE DEVOTIONS
OF LANCELOT ANDREWS BISHOP
OF WINCHESTER

TRANSLATED FROM THE GREEK AND LATIN
BY THE REV. PETER HALL M.A.
RECTOR OF MILSTON WILTS

TO WHICH IS ADDED THE MANUAL FOR THE SICK
BY THE SAME LEARNED PRELATE
SECOND EDITION CORRECTED

INSCRIPTION

UNDER A PORTRAIT OF THE AUTHOR.

IF EVER ANY MERITED TO BE
THE UNIVERSAL BISHOP, THIS WAS HE;
GREAT ANDREWS; WHO THE WHOLE VAST SEA DID DRAIN
OF LEARNING, AND DISTILL'D IT IN HIS BRAIN.
THESE PIOUS DROPS ARE OF THE PUREST KIND,
WHICH TRICKLED FROM THE LIMBECK OF HIS MIND.

ANOTHER.

THE LINEAMENTS OF ART HAVE WELL SET FORTH
SOME OUTWARD FEATURES, THOUGH NO INWARD WORTH,
BUT TO THESE LINES HIS WRITINGS ADDED, CAN
MAKE UP THE PAIR RESEMBLANCE OF A MAN.
FOR AS THE BODY'S FORM IS FIGUR'D HERE,
SO THERE THE BEAUTIES OF HIS SOUL APPEAR;
WHICH I HAD PRAISED, BUT THAT IN THIS PLACE
TO PRAISE HIM, WERE TO PRAISE HIM TO HIS FACE.

LONDON
C. WHITTINGHAM 21 TOOKS COURT
CHANCERY LANE

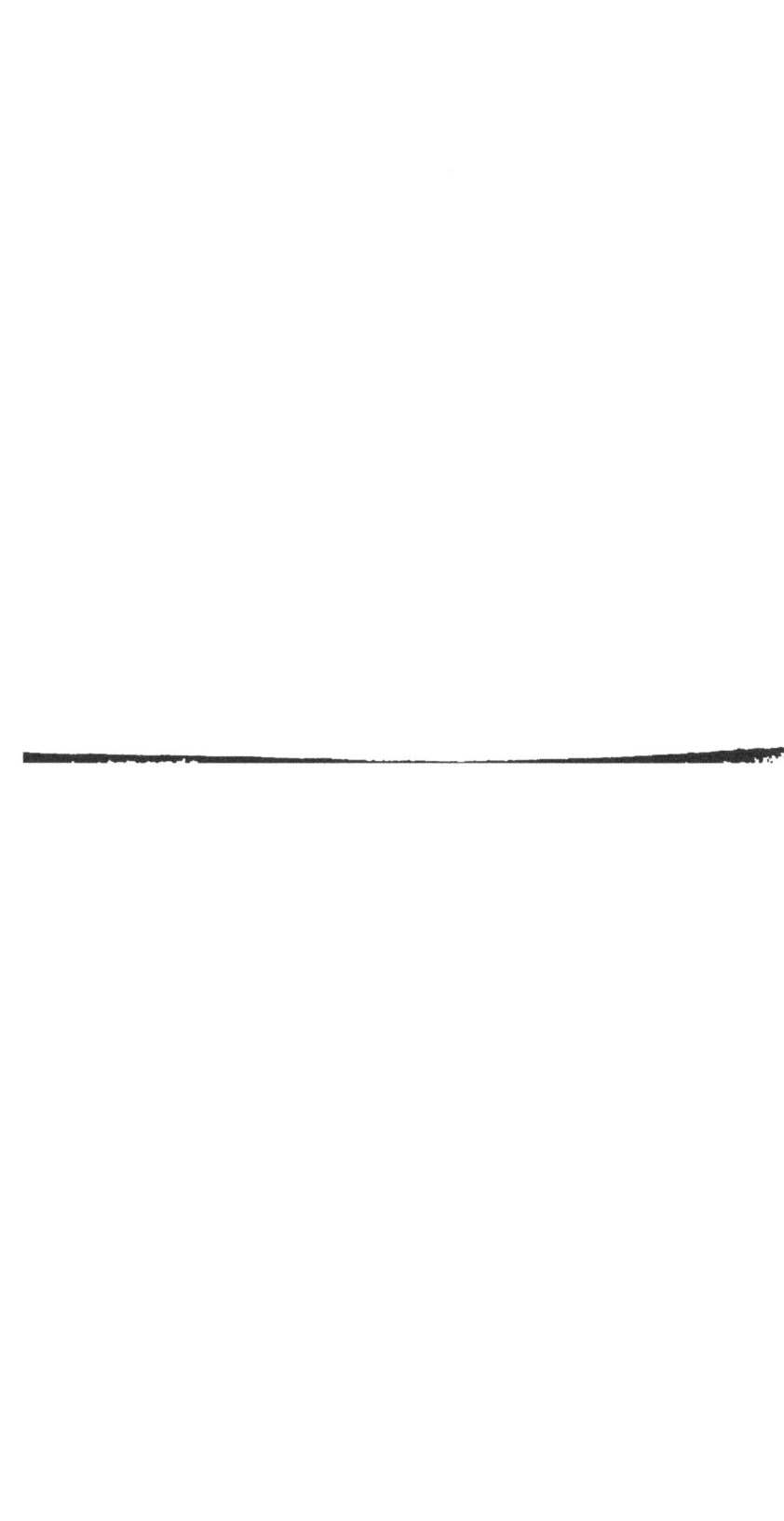

LANCELOT ANDREWS.
LORD BISHOP OF WINCHESTER
Natus 1554   Obiit 1626

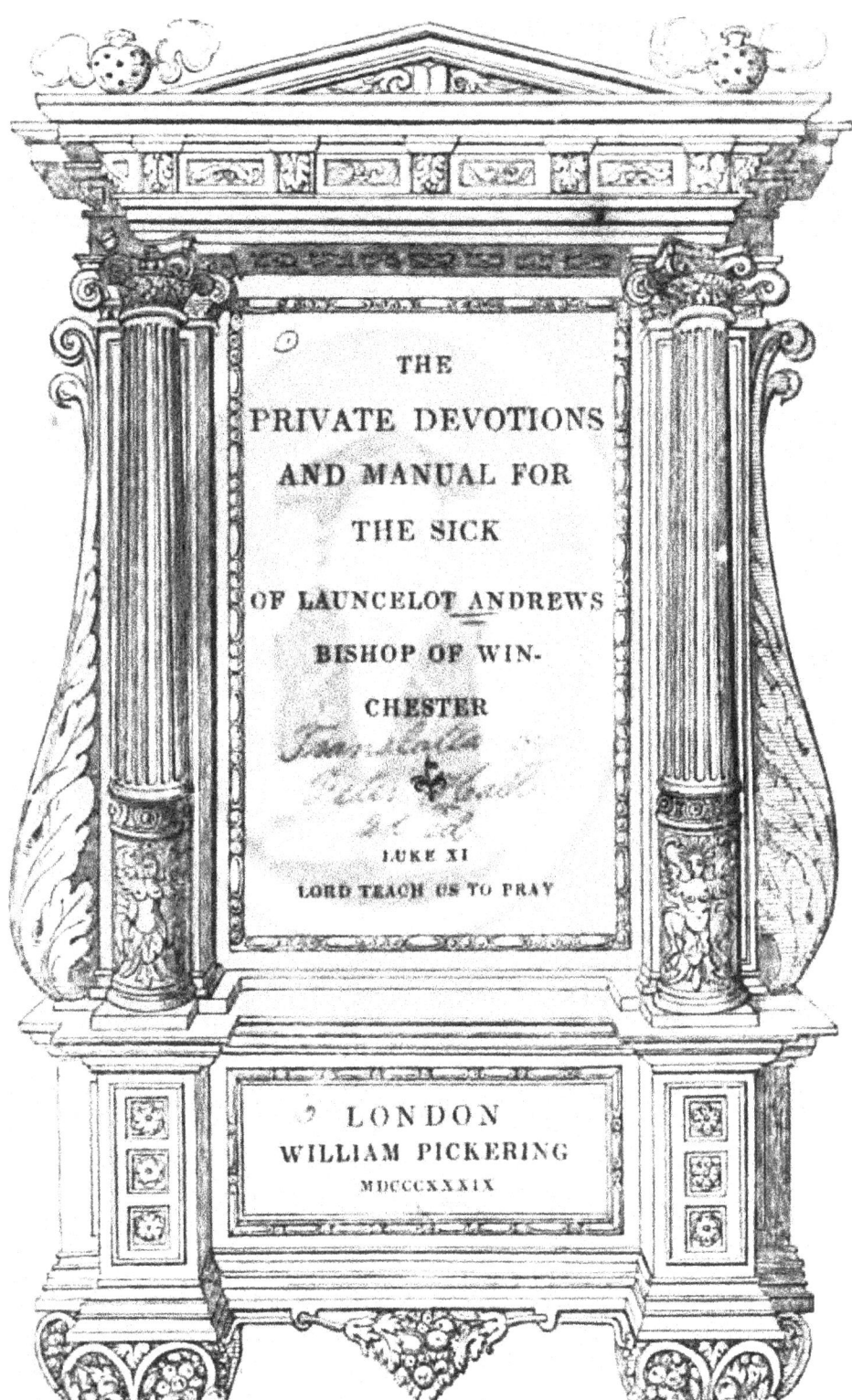

1860, July 13.
Pickman Bequest.

PREFACE TO THE FORMER EDITION.

It was at first the design of the translator to introduce the subject of his present labours with a minute inquiry into the life and character of that venerable being, the most beautiful of whose numerous productions he has here endeavoured to place in such a light, as should entitle them to more general acquaintance than heretofore. From the performance of this intention he has been withheld by the unexpected bulk to which the volume has extended, through the addition, not originally contemplated, of *the Manual for the Sick.* The necessity of this omission he has now the less reason to regret, since, in addition to the copious Memoir introduced by the Rev. S. H. Cassan into his *Lives of the Bishops of Winchester*, the valuable *Life of Andrews, by his Friend and Amanuensis, Henry Isaacson*, first published in 1650, incorporated the year following into *Fuller's Abel Redivivus*, and reprinted by John Trotter Brockett, Esq. of Newcastle, in 1817, has been lately edited with much diligence by the Rev. Stephen Isaacson, a lineal descendant of the writer.

Yet something it will be necessary to premise on this head, not merely to gratify the reader's inquisitiveness as to the history of the author and his work, but because many allusions occur throughout the latter, wholly inexplicable without a reference to the corresponding passages in the former.

Lancelot Andrews was born in the year 1555, in the parish of All-Hallows Barking, London. His father, who was master of Trinity House, and descended from an ancient and religious family in Suffolk, left his son in circumstances of respectability and comfort. The first rudiments of his education he received under Mr. Ward, in the Coopers' Free-School, at Ratcliffe; from whence he was removed to Merchant Tailors', at that time under the care of the celebrated Richard Mulcaster. Here his proficiency in the learned languages recommended him to the notice of Dr.

Thomas Watts, Prebendary of Westminster, and Archdeacon of Middlesex, who had just founded some scholarships at Pembroke Hall, Cambridge, and who bestowed upon young Andrews one of the earliest of those exhibitions.

Having proceeded to the degree of Bachelor of Arts, he was chosen, in 1576, a Fellow of his College, in preference to Mr. Dove, afterwards Bishop of Peterborough. Meanwhile, Jesus College, Oxford, had been founded by Hugh Price, who also appointed Andrews without delay to one of his Honorary Fellowships. As Master of Arts he now applied with signal success to the study of theological literature; and, independent of his reputation as a preacher and a casuist, the Lectures on the Commandments which he read, as catechist, to the undergraduates, procured him the admiration not only of his own associates, but of the University at large.

His next engagement was to accompany Henry, Earl of Huntingdon, President of the Council of York, into the north; where, by his zeal and eloquence, he gained over many recusants to the cause of Protestantism. From this circumstance his temporal advancement may be dated; for Sir Francis Walsingham, Secretary of State to Queen Elizabeth, hearing of his talents and activity, and unwilling that such deserts should linger in obscurity, bestowed on him the lease of Alton Parsonage, Hants, and afterwards procured for him the Vicarage of St. Giles's, Cripplegate, in London. He was soon after nominated a Canon Residentiary of St. Paul's, and Prebendary of the Collegiate Church of Southwell. On the death of Dr. Fulke, in 1589, he was chosen Master of Pembroke Hall, to which institution he afterwards became a considerable benefactor. He was chaplain in ordinary to Archbishop Whitgift, as well as to the Queen; the latter of whom appointed him, about the year 1595, a Prebendary of Westminster, and Dean about six years afterwards. He had also the honour of twice refusing a bishoprick in this reign, because he would not submit to a proposed alienation of their revenues from those of Salisbury and Ely, which were both offered to him.

The popularity of Dr. Andrews progressively increased

under the patronage of James the First, by whom he was commended to the see of Chichester, and to the office of Lord Almoner, in 1605; and further chosen to vindicate his sovereign against the malice and sophistry of his enemies. James, in his *Defence of the Rights of Kings*, had asserted the authority of Christian Princes over all causes and persons, ecclesiastical as well as civil. Cardinal Bellarmin, under the title of Matthew Tortus, attacked the King without scruple; but was answered by Andrews with much spirit, research, and judgment, according to Casaubon, in the *Tortura Torti*, published in 1609, and dedicated to his majesty. In reward for this good service, the writer was created a Privy Counsellor of England and Scotland; translated, the same year, to the see of Ely; and finally, in 1618, to that of Winchester; which, together with the Deanery of the Chapel Royal, he continued to hold, under favour of Charles the First, till the day of his death; an event which terminated a pious and valuable life of seventy-one years, on the 25th of September, 1626, at Winchester House, Southwark. His remains lie interred in the parish church of St. Saviour, under a handsome monument of marble and alabaster, erected by his executors, and distinguished by an appropriate inscription, in excellent Latin, from the pen of one of his chaplains. This monument was repaired in 1764; and on the bones of the departed prelate being accidentally disturbed, not many years ago, to make room for another corpse, the hair of his beard and his silken cap were found, among the relics of his coffin, undecayed.[*]

---

[*] In *Taylor's Annals of St. Mary Overy*, (1833, 4to.) the assertion here made is shewn to be inconsistent with the fact, that in 1830, on the removal of a chantry, which stood on the eastern side of the Lady Chapel connected with that venerable fabric, (now partly restored, and partly destroyed!) the coffin of the Bishop, bearing his initials, L. A., on the lid, was found unopened. Being not only made of lead, bandaged with a frame of iron, and attached by rings of the same material to a cross of brick-work, but closely and firmly entombed under an arch of stone, the coffin had sufficiently resisted the ravages of time to be carefully replaced in its cell, while the monument above was transferred to the back of the altar-screen.—P. H. 1839.

Such was the useful and honourable career of this most worthy father; and many have been the testimonies adduced to his virtues and attainments.—In *acts of piety, and devotional labour*, both public and domestic, it were almost impossible to name his superior; and of the purity of his heart abundant evidences survive in his writings, too disinterested to be mistaken for the fruit of any less holy motive. " His life," says a writer in the *Scholar Armed against the Errors of the Time*," was, in a great measure, a life of prayer; and his book of Private Devotions, composed in Greek and Latin for his own daily use, was, towards the conclusion of his life, scarcely ever out of his hands. In the time of his fever and last sickness, besides the prayers which were often read to him, in which he repeated the Confession and other parts with an audible voice so long as his strength served, he did, as was well observed by certain tokens in him, continually pray to himself, though he seemed otherwise to rest or slumber; and when he could pray no longer with his voice, by lifting up his eyes and hands he prayed still; and when they failed, he still prayed with his heart." Bishop Horne, alluding to the same volume of Devotions, says, " The manuscript was scarce ever out of his hands: it was found worn in pieces by his fingers, and wet with his tears." In the *Diary* of Archbishop Laud, he is emphatically denominated "The Light of the Christian World;" and that remarkable man is even represented to have adopted his private Ritual in administering the ceremonies of the church. With still more energy he is characterised by the editor of his *Holy Devotions*, as " Doctor Andrews in the schools, Bishop Andrews in the pulpit, and Saint Andrews in the closet."—His *charity* was great, even when he was poor; but in the days of his wealth it grew to be unbounded: he released the prisoner from his cell, he clothed the naked, he fed the hungry, he gave medicines to the sick. All this he did without even the lawful hope of gratitude; for those who received his alms were never made acquainted with the giver: and his will, of which some portions will be found in *Gutch's Collectanea Curiosa*, evinces the desire he entertained to extend his benefactions, when personally removed from all further chances of acknowledgment.—His *integrity* in the various offices confided to his charge was incorruptible; and it is believed that the sums he was appointed to distribute in the name of others, were ever secretly augmented by his own private bounty. What opinion Lord Clarendon held of his honesty and fidelity may be gathered from the remark he makes, in recording the decease of Archbishop Bancroft, that " If he had been succeeded by Bishop Andrews, or any man who understood and loved the church, that infection would easily have been kept out, which could not afterwards be so easily expelled." And a greater compliment could hardly have been paid by a more upright man, than that of an Elegy, from the pen of Milton, on a prelate, the avowed defender of regal prerogative. Usury, simony, and sacrilege, were the three crimes which above all others he abhorred; ascribing to them most of those evils which had at various seasons afflicted and disgraced the church.—In witness of his *gratitude*, it is known that he bestowed on Dr. Ward, the son of his first schoolmaster, the valuable rectory of Bishops-Waltham, Hants; that to Mr. Mulcaster he always manifested the most respectful regard, and placed his portrait over his own study-door; and that he caused the Fellowships he founded at Pembroke Hall, Cambridge, to be first supplied out of the Scholarships endowed at the same college by Dr. Watts, and bequeathed a perpetual provision for the kindred of his early patron.—His *bounty* induced him to receive the applications of strangers in distress with a perpetual welcome; while the splendour of his entertainments to King James, both at Farnham Castle, and in his journey into Scotland, procured him a reputation for hospitality unparalleled but in the royal progresses of that monarch. And whatever office he undertook, whatever mansion he inhabited, he was sure to leave in a better condition than that in which it came into his hands.—His *affability* and *condescension* not only won him the esteem of all who entered into his presence, but engaged him in correspondence with many of the first scholars at that day in Europe; particularly with Casaubon, Cluverius, Vossius, Grotius, Peter de Moulin,

Barclay, and Erpenius.—In reference to his *literary attainments*, he is called by Boisius, in the preface to his *Collation of the Old Interpreters*, " A stupendous miracle and oracle of our age; in languages a Mithridates; in arts an Aristotle; and so in his own person embracing all accomplishments, that while others have been content with one, he has in himself comprised them all." In the Conference of Hampton Court, his name stands first upon the list of those, to whom the new translation of the Bible was committed; and it is asserted by Buckeridge, Bishop of Rochester, who preached the sermon at his funeral, that he was competent to the reading of no less than fifteen languages.—In his *pastoral* and *episcopal* duties, he was exact and indefatigable; searching at the universities for young men of promise, and rewarding them according to their proficiency and diligence. Presiding, as visitor, by his station in the church, over several colleges and public schools, he exerted himself to maintain impartiality in the elections and presentations of those societies.—Yet with these, and many other tokens of a Christian disposition, let not his *humility* be overlooked, in the motto he selected, at his consecration, to be engraven on his seal, from 2 Cor. ii. 16. " Who is sufficient for these things ?"

And now, to adopt the language of his first Biographer, " let us lay all these together: his zeal and piety; his charity and compassion; his fidelity and integrity; his gratitude and thankfulness; his munificence and bounty; hospitality, humanity, affability, and modesty; and to these his indefatigability in study, and the fruits of his labours in his sermons and writings, together with his profundity in all kinds of learning; his wit, memory, judgment, gravity, and humility; his detestation of all vices and sins, but especially of three; and consider, whether the Church of God in general, and this in particular, did not suffer an irreparable loss by his death."—*Isaacson's Memoir*, 1829. pp. 56, 7.

Till the very last year of his life the perceptions of his great mind continued unimpaired, and his diligence unabated. "He was not often sick," continues Mr. Isaacson; "but once, indeed, till his last sickness, in thirty years before the time he died; which was at Downham, in the Isle of Ely. But there he seemed to be prepared for his dissolution, saying oftentimes in that sickness, "It must come once; why not here?" and at other times, before and since, he would say, "The days must come, when, whether we will or nill, we shall say with the Preacher, (Eccles. vii. 1.) I have no pleasure in them."—p. 57.

"After the death of his brother, Mr. Thomas Andrews, in the sickness-time, whom he dearly loved,"—(the anecdote is from his funeral sermon,)—"he began to foretell his own death before the end of summer, or before the beginning of winter. And when his brother, Mr. Nicholas Andrews, died, he took that as a certain sign and prognostic, and warning of his own death. And from that time, until the hour of his dissolution, he spent all his time in prayer, until it pleased God to receive his blessed soul to himself."

To return once more to the pages of his amiable Amanuensis. "As he lived, so died he. As his fidelity in his health was great, so increased the strength of his faith in his sickness: his gratitude to men was now changed into his thankfulness to God; his affability, to incessant and devout prayers and speech with his Creator, Redeemer, and Sanctifier; his laborious studies, to his restless groans, sighs, cries, and tears; his hands labouring; his eyes lifted up; and his heart beating and panting to see the living God, even to the last of his breath. And him, no doubt, he sees face to face, his works preceding and following him, and he now following the Lamb, crowned with that immortality, which is reserved for every one who lives such a life as he lived."—pp. 57, 8.

At what period of his ministry the contents of the ensuing pages were composed, can scarcely be at this time ascertained. The *Manual for the Sick* he is generally supposed to have employed in the visitation of his parishioners at St. Giles's, Cripplegate: but that the *Private Devotions* were written, or at least in some parts modified, at a later day, is

LANCELOT ANDREWS.
LORD BISHOP OF WINCHESTER
Natus 1555 Obiit 1626.

writer's family and situation, are retained, chiefly as matters of curiosity; they will be easily altered to an agreement with the wants and circumstances of the reader.

"By the best judgment I can make of this book," says Mr. Hutton, in his Preface, "Bishop Andrews appears to have collected, from time to time, in the course of his reading, materials for every part of prayer; which he wrote down, some in Greek, and some in Latin. These at first were chiefly hints; but out of them he composed several prayers, that he used privately in his closet, and some of them publicly in the Church, before sermon, having translated them into English. Many of these prayers were completely finished, and used by him as forms; in others he left some hints, not quite completed, but wherein it was easy for him to supply all that was wanting, as he used them. These he varied often, as occasion and necessity required, and improved them by degrees. Such of them as were brought nearest to perfection, he wrote in Greek; either because the New Testament, Septuagint, and most ancient Fathers and Liturgies (whence he extracted a great deal) were in that language; or because that language has some advantage for devotion, as the many compound words it contains, strengthen the ideas they convey to us, and make a more lively impression upon the mind."

"Dean Stanhope," he continues, "who often used these devotions in the original language, and had committed a good part of them to his memory, was so well pleased with them, that he took the pains to translate what is contained in the following sheets, for the use of a dear friend, to whom he apprehended they would be acceptable and serviceable. They gave so great satisfaction, and did so much service, not only to that friend, but to all those into whose hands the copies came, that the Dean resolved, I suppose at their desire, to print them."

Among the posthumous papers of Bishop Horne, besides a corrected copy of Dean Stanhope's Version, was discovered one, now probably lost, which, if published at the time, might have superseded some portion of the present translator's labours. "In the copy published after Dean Stanhope's form," says the Rev. William Jones, in his *Memoirs* of that Bishop, " *The Manual for the Sick*, though the best thing extant upon its subject, is wholly omitted; but in the posthumous manuscript I speak of, the whole is put together, with improvements by the compiler; and I wish all the parochial clergy in the nation were possessed of it."

To supply, in some measure, this public loss, has been now, with conscious incapacity, attempted. In lack of the original composition, no other resource presented itself to the editor, but carefully to compare the references, inserted by Dr. Drake, and such others as occurred to himself, with the authorities referred to; so that, if in any instance the words of Bishop Andrews should be lost sight of, those of a greater authority than he, and one to which he ever bowed himself with the deepest humility, might be substituted in their stead.

At the conclusion of this Manual will be found two prayers, extracted from a MS. volume in possession of the publisher, and containing, among other devotional formularies, a great number of those compiled by our author. It is subscribed, " November 13, 1643; in the second year of the civil war of England; by T. N."

Of the other works of Lancelot Andrews, the best known are his Sermons, first published in 1628, fol. of which seventeen have been edited by the late Archdeacon Daubeny; seven, on the Temptation, by the Rev. William Kirby; and nineteen, on Prayer, have been just announced by Mr. Edward Williams. " He was, without exception," says the writer before quoted, in the *Scholar Armed*, " the first preacher of his time; and his discourses and lectures, though somewhat obsolete from their antiquity in style and manner, are yet so excellent for the truth, learning, eloquence, and piety, found in them, that when we have laid down rules for a preacher, no character can be produced, in which they were better exemplified." He was also author of an *Exposition on the Ten Commandments*, 1642, fol.; *Posthumous and Orphan Lectures*, 1657, fol.; and *Holy Devotions, with*

Directions to Pray, of which the fourth edition appeared in 1655, and the fifth in 1633, 12mo.* He is supposed to have had some hand in the *Chronological History* of Mr. Isaacson; of which an enlarged and corrected edition is promised by the same gentleman, who has just republished his Memoir of the Bishop. His *Miscellaneous Works* were printed in a 4to. volume in 1629, by order of Charles the First, to whom they are inscribed by Laud Bishop of London, and Buckeridge of Ely, the contemporaries and friends of the deceased. In the library of Trinity College, Dublin, is preserved a MS. volume, in Latin, attributed to Bishop Andrews, on the *Form of Government in the Old and New Testament*; a disquisition on which subject, in English, is appended to the volume of MS. Prayers, before alluded to, though printed at Oxford, in 1641, fol. And as it is not impossible there may be other remains of the same gifted writer in other collections, though hitherto unknown or unappropriated, it may be well to mention that facsimiles of his autograph appear in *Mr. Whitaker's History of Craven*, as well as in the recent collection by Mr. Nichols.

Original paintings of Bishop Andrews are preserved at Pembroke Hall, Cambridge, and in the Bodleian Gallery at Oxford. His engraved portraits are very numerous; 1st, by Simon Pass, as Bishop of Ely, 1616; 2nd, by the same, as Bishop of Winton, 1618, copied by Vertue; 3rd, by Payne, prefixed to his *Sermons* and *Exposition of the Commandments*, copied for Drake, and for the present volume; 4th, by Hollar, in *Sparrow's Rationale of the Common Prayer*, copied by Loggan, for the *Preces Privatæ*, 1675; by Simpson, for Stanhope; and by Walker, for Mr. Isaacson's reprint.

But it is now time to close this introduction, and admit the reader to the enjoyment of a devotional exercise, prepared for his soul's health and edification. " The heart,

---

* This little volume was first published in 1630, under the title of Institutiones Piæ ; the three first impressions having the signature, H. I. (conjectured to be Henry Isaacson) subjoined. A new edition is just announced by the Rev. W. H. Hale, Preacher of the Charter-House.—P. H. 1830.

already enlightened and inflamed," says Mr. Hutton, "with piety and charity, will here find something exactly suitable to its inward motions, and the most significant and beautiful words, wherein to utter its holy desires, and those gracious sentiments, which, without this help, would perhaps break forth with less advantage, and less accuracy both of method and expression. But the less perfect Christian, who has not yet made so much progress in the school of piety as the former, may reap still greater benefit from this work. It will tend to improve him in knowledge and practice; it will be, to such, an excellent Catechism, as well as a Prayer Book; he will here find the Commandments and the Creed, and other important points of Christian instruction, explained and applied with great judgment, and no less perspicuity than brevity; so that they may be soon learnt, and easily remembered. He may here be led to form just notions and holy desires, such as cannot but have a considerable influence on his prayers and his manners. He will be put in mind of the variety and greatness of his sins, and of his wants; of the holiness, the mercy, and the goodness of God, and the many invaluable benefits he heaps on mankind. In short, by a serious and proper use of this Manual, he will perceive himself to advance apace in love to God and man, and every other Christian grace and virtue."

Approach then, pious reader, (be it permitted to exclaim,) with a teachable and contrite heart; and the Spirit of God be with thee. " Enter into thy closet, and shut thy door (Matt. vi. 6.); pray with Bishop Andrews for one week; and he will be pleasant in thy life; and at the hour of death he will not forsake thee."

Ringwood, Hants.
November 25th, 1829.

Lately Published, by WILLIAM PICKERING, *Chancery Lane.*

LANCELOTI ANDREWS, EPISCOPI WINTONIENSIS, PRECES PRIVATÆ QUOTIDIANÆ, Græcè et Latinè. A new Edition, carefully revised and corrected, by the Rev. Peter Hall, M. A. Rector of Milston, Wilts. 18mo. 12s.

THE WORKS OF THE REV. GEORGE HERBERT.
Now first collected. In 2 vols. foolscap 8vo. with Portrait, and View of Bemerton Church, 10s.

The POEMS contain The Temple; (the Synagogue, by the Rev. Christopher Harvey;) the Latin Poems of Herbert; and two Original Poems, never before printed. With Notes by S. T. COLERIDGE.

The REMAINS contain the Priest to the Temple, Proverbs, and other Prose Works, including many pieces never before printed, with his Life by IZAAK WALTON, and also that by his first biographer, BARNABAS OLEY.

GOOD THOUGHTS IN BAD TIMES, Good Thoughts in Worse Times, Mixt Contemplations in better Times, by THOMAS FULLER, D.D., Author of the Church History, Worthies of England, &c. 18mo. with a Portrait, 5s.

SIBBES'S SOUL'S CONFLICT. Foolscap 8vo. 5s.

SIBBES'S BRUISED REED. To which is added, "A FOUNTAIN SEALED," and "A DESCRIPTION OF CHRIST." Fcap. 8vo. 5s.

⁎ The writings of Sibbes were much admired by Izaak Walton, who in his last will says, "I give to my son, Dr. Sibbes' *Soul's Conflict,* and to my daughter, his *Bruised Reed,* desiring them to read them so as to become acquainted with them;" and in another place, Walton says:—

"Of this blest man let this just praise be given,
Heaven was in him, before he was in heaven."

PRACTICAL DISCOURSES ON ALL THE PARTS AND OFFICES OF THE LITURGY OF THE CHURCH OF ENGLAND, by the REV. MATTHEW HOLE. A New Edition, in 4 vols. 8vo. 2l. 2s.

SELECTIONS FROM THE WORKS OF TAYLOR, HOOKER, BARROW, SOUTH, LATIMER, BROWNE, MILTON, AND BACON. By BASIL MONTAGU, Esq. Fourth edition, foolscap 8vo. 5s.

TABLE OF CONTENTS.

I. DAILY PRAYERS. FIRST PART.

	Page
SEASONS OF PRAYER	3
PLACES OF PRAYER	4
INTERCESSIONS	5
PREPARATORY PRAYERS	5
AT ENTRANCE INTO THE CHURCH	5
CONFESSIONS	6
HEADS OF PRAYER	8
GESTURES OF THE BODY	10
MORNING PRAYER	11
EJACULATIONS AND PRAYERS FOR THE CHAMBER	14
SUNDAY	19
An Act of Confession	20
A Prayer for Grace	24
The Fence of the Law	26
An Act of Faith	26
An Act of Intercession	30
An Act of Praise	37
MONDAY	39
An Act of Confession	39
A Prayer for Grace	41
The Apostles' Creed	42
An Act of Intercession	43
An Act of Praise	47
TUESDAY	49
An Act of Confession	49
A Prayer for Grace	51

CONTENTS.

	Page
An Act of Faith	51
An Act of Intercession	52
The Attributes of Mercy	54

WEDNESDAY 56
    An Act of Confession 56
    An Act of Faith 59
    An Act of Intercession 61
    An Act of Praise 67

THURSDAY 68
    An Act of Confession 68
    A Prayer for Grace 70
    An Act of Faith 71
    An Act of Intercession 72
    An Act of Praise 74

FRIDAY 77
    An Act of Contrition 78
    A Prayer for Grace 81
    An Act of Faith 82
    An Act of Intercession 83
    An Act of Praise 85

SATURDAY 87
    An Act of Confession 87
    A Prayer for Grace 88
    An Act of Faith 90
    An Act of Intercession 92
    An Act of Praise 93

A FORM OF PRAYER FOR ALL THE WORLD 95
A RECOMMENDATION TO GOD'S BLESSING 96
PRAYERS, PREPARATORY TO THANKSGIVING 97
A FORM OF THANKSGIVING 97
A LITANY, or DEPRECATION 100
HOSANNA IN THE HIGHEST 106
HOSANNA UPON EARTH 108

EVENING PRAYERS AND MEDITATIONS 111
    A Confession of Sin 112
    At the Approach of Night 115
    At Bed-time 117
    A Prayer for All Estates 118

PRAYERS FOR THE HOLY COMMUNION 120

	Page
SPECIAL DUTIES OF CHRISTIAN PEOPLE	126
MEDITATION 1. ON THE DAY OF JUDGMENT	128
2. ON THE FRAILTY OF HUMAN LIFE	131

II. DAILY PRAYERS. SECOND PART.

A GENERAL CONFESSION	137
MORNING PRAYERS	140
A General Supplication	143
An Act of Thanksgiving	146
A Deprecation against Wrath to come	151
AN EVENING SACRIFICE	155
The Horology, or Dial of Prayer	155
Appeals to the Deity	161
A Confession of Praise	171
THE PASSION OF OUR LORD	176
A CONFESSION OF SIN	179
AN ACT OF INTERCESSION	184
AN ACT OF PRAISE	190
THE LORD'S PRAYER, PARAPHRASED	195
PRAYERS FOR THE HOUSE OF GOD	201
PRAYER ON GOING A JOURNEY	204
THE PRAYER OF ARCHBISHOP BRADWARDINE	206
AN ACT OF ADORATION	208
A PRAYER FOR DELIVERANCE	209
AN ACT OF HOPE	210
A DOXOLOGY	213
HYMN 1. FOR THE MORNING	217
2. FOR THE EVENING	218
CHRIST CRUCIFIED, A MONOSTROPHIC	218

III. MANUAL FOR THE SICK.

Preparatory Admonitions	223
Inquiries to be made concerning the Sick Party	223
General Considerations of the Mortality of Man	224
Comfortable Scriptures to be used to the Sick	224
Several Duties recommended to the Sick	228
Propositions and Inferences to be made to the Sick	230

	Page
Prayers and Expressions of the Soul's Affiance in God .	238
A Commendation of the Sick to the Blessed Trinity ...	240
A Profession of Christianity by the Sick	242
Heads of Comfort, from the Consideration of God and Christ	243
A Collection of Prayers, chiefly from the Psalter.........	244
A Prayer by the Priest, begging Pardon for his own Unworthiness	257
A Litany for the Sick Person, when in danger of Death	258
An humble Recognition of Human Frailty	264
An affectionate Recommendation of the Sick to God's Mercy	264
A Prayer for Mercy and Divine Assistance...............	267
A Prayer for Grace and Pardon.............................	269
A Commendation of the Soul to God	271
Comfortable Scriptures to Friends of the Deceased	273
A General Confession of Sins	273
A Confession of Sins, according to the Decalogue	278
The Triumph of Mercy	282
Spiritual Comfort and Confidence	289
Devout Ejaculations	290
APPENDIX 1. *A Prayer for the King*	293
2. *A Prayer in Times of War*..................	295

DAILY PRAYERS AND MEDITATIONS.

PART THE FIRST.

"The best arrangement of all our conversations, and of all our actions, is to begin with God, and to end in God."—*Gregory Nazianzen.*

"Think not lightly of thy prayers, for He who heareth them thinketh not lightly of them; but even before they are passed from thy lips, He hath them written in His own book. And one of these two things we ought steadfastly to hope: that He will grant either that which we desire, or that which He knows to be more profitable to us."—*St. Bernard.*

DAILY PRAYERS AND MEDITATIONS.

FIRST PART.

SEASONS OF PRAYER.

ALWAYS.—*Luke* xviii. 1.

Without ceasing.—1 *Thes.* v. 17.

At all times.—*Ephes.* vi. 18.

He kneeled upon his knees three times a day, and prayed, and gave thanks before his God, as he did aforetime.—*Dan.* vi. 10.

Evening, and morning, and at noon, will I pray, and cry aloud; and he shall hear my voice.—*Ps.* lv. 17.

Seven times a day do I praise thee.—*Psalm* cxix. 164.

  1. In the morning, a great while before day.—*Mark* i. 35.

  2. In the night watches.—*Psalm* lxiii. 6.

  3. At the third hour of the day.—*Acts* ii. 15.

  4. About the sixth hour.—*Acts* x. 9.

  5. At the hour of prayer, being the ninth hour.—*Acts* iii. 1.

  6. At the eventide.—*Gen.* xxiv. 63.

7. By night.—*Psalm* cxxxiv. 1.

At midnight.—*Psalm* cxix. 62 ; *Acts* xvi. 25.

PLACES OF PRAYER.

In all places where I record my name, I will come unto thee, and I will bless thee.—*Exod.* xx. 24.

Congregation.

In the assembly of the upright, and in the congregation.—*Psalm* cxi. 1.

Closet.

Enter into thy closet, and, when thou hast shut thy door, pray to thy Father, which is in secret.—*Matt.* vi. 6.

House-top.

He went up upon the house-top to pray.—*Acts* x. 9.

Temple.

They went up into the temple.—*Acts* iii. 1.

Sea-shore.

We kneeled down on the shore.—*Acts* xxi. 5.

Garden.

He entered into the garden to pray.—*John* xviii. 1. *Matt.* xxvi. 36.

Bed.

Upon their bed.—*Psalm* cxlix. 5.

Wilderness.

He withdrew himself into the wilderness, and prayed.—*Luke* v. 16; *Mark* i. 35.

Pray *every where*, lifting up holy hands, without wrath and doubting.—1 *Tim.* ii. 8.

INTERCESSIONS.

SAMUEL, among them that called upon his name.
—*Psalm* xcix. 6.

As for me, God forbid that I should sin against the Lord in ceasing to pray for you: but I will teach you the good and the right way.—1 *Samuel* xii. 23.

But we will give ourselves continually to prayer, and to the ministry of the word.—*Acts* vi. 4.

PREPARATORY PRAYERS.

O THOU that hearest prayer, unto thee shall all flesh come (*Ps.* lxv. 2.): even my flesh shall come.

Iniquities prevail against me: as for our transgressions, thou shalt purge them away.—*Verse* 3.

O Lord, open thou my lips, and my mouth shall shew forth thy praise.—*Psalm* xi. 15.

AT ENTRANCE INTO THE CHURCH.

As for me, I will come into thy house in the multitude of thy mercy; and in thy fear will I worship toward thy holy temple.—*Psalm* v. 7.

Hear the voice of my supplications, when I cry unto thee; when I lift up my hands toward thy holy oracle.—*Psalm* xxviii. 2.

We have thought of thy loving-kindness, O God, in the midst of thy temple.—*Ps.* xlviii. 9.

Be mindful, O Lord, of the brethren who are present with us, and who pray with us at this time:

be mindful of their devotion and their zeal. Be mindful of those also, who upon good cause are absent; and have mercy upon them and us, according to the multitude of thy mercies, O Lord.

LET us bless thee for our godly princes, orthodox prelates, the founders of this sacred institution.

Glory be to thee, O Lord, glory be to thee : glory be to thee, because thou hast glorified them, for whom we also glorify thee.

Let, I beseech thee, thine eyes be open, and let thine ears be attent unto the prayer which thy servant prayeth toward this place, which is called by thy name.—2 *Chron.* vi. 40. 20. 33.

CONFESSIONS.

WOE is me! I have sinned against thee, O Lord, I have sinned against thee; I have perverted that which was right, and it profited me not.—*Job* xxxiii. 27.

But I am ashamed, and turn from my wicked ways, and return unto my own heart, and with my whole heart return unto thee.

And I seek thy face, and I beseech thee, saying :

I have sinned, I have done perversely, I have committed wickedness.—1 *Kings* viii. 47.

Lord, I feel the anguish of my heart;

And, behold, I return unto thee with all my heart, and with all my soul.—*Verse* 48.

And now, O Lord, from Heaven, from thy dwelling-place on high, from thy throne of glory in thy heavenly kingdom, hear thou the prayer and supplication of thy servant, and be merciful to thy servant, and heal his soul.—1 *Kings* viii. 28. 30; *Psalm* xli. 4.

I dare not lift up so much as mine eyes unto Heaven, but, standing afar off, I smite upon my breast, and say, with the Publican,

God be merciful to me a sinner;—*Luke* xviii. 13.
To me, a greater sinner than the Publican;
To me be merciful, as to the Publican.

THE wrath of man shall praise thee: the remainder of wrath shalt thou restrain.—*Ps.* lxxvi. 10.

I have sinned.   I confess.

Have mercy on me, $\begin{cases} \text{according to.} \\ \text{by, and for the sake of.} \\ \text{inasmuch as.} \end{cases}$

I offer up myself.   I am weak.

Assist me, $\begin{cases} \text{by.} \\ \text{in.} \end{cases}$

Lord, I believe; help thou mine unbelief.—*Mark* ix. 24.

Lord, increase my faith.—*Luke* xvii. 5.

And now, Lord, what wait I for? My hope is in thee.—*Psalm* xxxix. 7.

Enlighten mine eyes, and I shall understand; incline my heart, and I will love thee; direct my steps, and I will walk in the way of thy commandments.

HEADS OF PRAYER.

Let us entreat the Lord, in behalf of
1. The Creation.
   The human race.
   The sick.
2. The Catholic Church.
   The Eastern Church.
   The Western Church.
   The Church of England.
3. Bishops.
   Priests.
   Deacons.
   Christian people.
   Christians of our own country.
4. The kingdoms of the world.
   Christian kingdoms.
   Neighbouring kingdoms.
   Our own.
5. Those whom it hath pleased God to elect Kings.
   Our own King.
   His Privy Council.
   The Judges.
   Magistrates.
   Army and Navy.
   Community at large.
   Our Youth.
   Our Places of Education.
         With regard to
6. The nature of man.

The obligation of benefits received.
The supply of our daily wants.
Matters entrusted to our charge.

At some former period; as, in my case,
- My College.
- My Parish.
- Southwell.
- St. Paul's.
- Westminster.
- Chichester.
- Ely.

At this present time; as,
- The Diocese of Winchester.
- My Chapel.
- My Church.
- The Chapel Royal.
- The disbursement of the King's alms.
- My six Colleges.

7. Moral friendship.
Christian charity.
Vicinity of situation.
A promise.
Mutual duty.
Weight of business.
Paucity of intercessors.

    For those who labour under difficulties.

    For those who have any important undertaking at hand.

    For those who have at any time been hindered by my interference.

Halleluja. Hosanna in the highest.
Hosanna upon earth. Halleluja.

GESTURES OF THE BODY,

DENOTING THE AFFECTIONS OF THE MIND.

1. Bowing the knees,　　　Humiliation.
    He kneeled down.—*Luke* xxii. 41.
    He fell on his face.—*Matt.* xxvi. 39.

    Our soul is bowed down to the dust:
    Our belly cleaveth unto the earth.—*Ps.* xliv. 25.
2. Bowing the head,
    Hanging down the coun-
        tenance,　　　　　　Confusion.
3. Smiting the breast,　　Indignation.
4. Trembling,　　　　　　Fear.
5. Groaning,
    Wringing the hands,　　Sorrow.
6. Lifting up the eyes
    And hands,　　　　　　Vehement desire.
7. Striking violently,　　　Revenge.
    　　　　See 2 *Cor.* vii. 11.

MORNING PRAYER.

GLORY be to thee, O Lord, glory be to thee: glory to thee, who hast given me sleep to refresh my weakness, and to alleviate the labours of this fragile flesh.

That this day, and every day, we may pass in the perfecting of holiness, (2 *Cor.* vii. 1.) in peace, health, and innocence,

    Grant us, O Lord.

That the angel of peace, our faithful guide, the guardian of our souls and bodies, may encamp round about us, (*Psalm* xxxiv. 7.) and continually suggest what is needful for our salvation,

    Grant us, O Lord.

The pardon and remission of all our sins and all our transgressions,

    Grant us, O Lord.

To our souls what is good and profitable, and to the world peace,

    Grant us, O Lord.

That we may accomplish the remainder of our lives in penitence and godly fear, in health of body and peace of mind,

    Grant us, O Lord.

Whatsoever things are true, whatsoever things are honest, whatsoever things are just, whatsoever things are pure, whatsoever things are lovely, whatsoever things are of good report; if there be any virtue, and if there be any praise, (*Philip.* iv. 8.) that we may think on these things, and do them,

Grant us, O Lord.

A Christian termination of our lives, free from sin and shame, and, if such be thy pleasure, free from pain, and a good account of ourselves before the dread and terrible tribunal of our Lord Jesus Christ,

Grant us, O Lord.
(*See Liturgy of St. Chrysostom.*)

O BEING, above all beings, O uncreated Nature,
Thou Framer of the universe,—*Col.* i. 16, 17.
I set thee, Lord, always before me;—*Ps.* xvi. 8.
Unto thee do I lift up my soul.—*Ps.* xxv. 1.
I worship and bow down before thee;—*Psalm* xcv. 6.
I humble myself under thy mighty hand.—1 *Pet.* v. 6.
I stretch forth my hands unto thee;
My soul thirsteth after thee, as a thirsty land.—*Psalm* cxliii. 6.
I smite upon my breast,
And I say, with the publican,
God, be merciful to me, a sinner altogether;—*Luke* xviii. 13.
To me, the chief of sinners;—1 *Tim.* i. 15.
To me, a greater sinner than the publican,
Be merciful, as to the publican.

O FATHER of mercies,
I beseech thee by thy fatherly bowels of compassion, (1 *John* iii. 17.) despise me not,
    An unclean worm;—*Psalm* xxii. 6.
    A dead dog;—2 *Sam.* ix. 8.
    A stinking carcase.—*John* xi. 39.
Forsake not the work of thine own hands;—*Psalm* cxxxviii. 8.
Forsake not thine own image,—*Gen.* i. 27.
Though bearing the marks of iniquity.—*Gen.* iv. 15.
Lord, if thou wilt, thou canst make me clean;
Lord, speak the word only, and I shall be healed.—*Matt.* viii. 2. 8.

AND THOU, my Saviour, Christ,
O Christ, my Saviour,
Saviour of sinners, of whom I am chief;—1 *Tim.* i. 15.
Despise me not,
Despise me not, O Lord.
Despise not the purchase of thine own blood,
The pledge of thine own name;
O Lord, despise me not.
But rather look on me with those thine eyes,
With which thou lookedst
On Mary Magdalene at the banquet,
On Peter in the High Priest's palace,
On the malefactor upon the cross;

That, with the malefactor, I may humbly call upon thee,

Lord, remember me in thy kingdom :—*Luke* xxiii. 42.

With Peter, I may weep bitterly, (*Matt.* xxvi. 75.) and say,

O! that mine eyes were a fountain of tears, that I might weep day and night ;—*Jer.* ix. 1.

With Magdalene, I may hear thee say,

Thy sins are forgiven thee ;

And that, with her, I may love much, because many and manifold are the sins forgiven me.—*Luke* vii. 47, 48.

AND THOU, all-holy, gracious, and quickening Spirit, despise me not,

A creature of thine own inspiring,

An object of thine own sanctifying;

Despise me not.

But return, O Lord, how long? and let it repent thee concerning thy servant.—*Psalm* xc. 13.

EJACULATIONS AND PRAYERS FOR THE CHAMBER.

BLESSED art thou, O Lord our God, the God of our fathers, who turnest the shadow of death into the morning, (*Amos* v. 8.) and renewest the face of the earth.—*Psalm* civ. 30.

Who scatterest darkness from the face of light;

who separatest the night, and bringest back the day;

Who hast lightened mine eyes, lest I should sleep the sleep of death.—*Psalm* xiii. 3.

Who hast delivered me from the terror by night, from the pestilence that walketh in darkness.—*Psalm* xci. 5, 6.

Who hast withdrawn sleep from mine eyes, and slumber from mine eyelids.—*Psalm* cxxxii. 4.

Who makest the outgoings of the morning and evening to rejoice.—*Psalm* lxv. 8.

For that I laid me down, and slept; I awaked; for thou, Lord, sustainedst me.—*Psalm* iii. 5.

I awaked, and beheld; and my sleep was sweet unto me.—*Jer.* xxxi. 26.

BLOT out, O Lord, as a thick cloud, my transgressions, and dispel, as a morning cloud, my sins.—*Isaiah* xliv. 22.

Grant that I may be a child of light, and a child of the day:—1 *Thess.* v. 5.

That I may walk soberly, chastely, and honestly, as in the day.—*Rom.* xiii. 13.

Vouchsafe to keep me this day without sin.—*Te Deum.*

Thou that upholdest all that fall, and raisest up all those that be bowed down;—*Psalm* cxlv. 14.

Grant that I may never harden my heart (*Ps.* xcv. 8.) under provocation or temptation, or through any deceitfulness of sin.—*Heb.* iii. 8. 13.

Moreover, deliver me this day,
  From the snare of the fowler,
  From the noisome pestilence,
  From the arrow that flieth by day,
  From evil and mischief,
  From the destruction that wasteth at noonday.—*Psalm* xci. 3. 5. 6.

Preserve this day from any evil of mine, and me from the evil of this day.—*Matt.* vi. 34.

Let not my days be consumed in vanity, nor my years in trouble.—*Psalm* lxxviii. 33.

Let one day utter speech unto another.—*Ps.* xix. 2.

Let this day add somewhat, in knowledge or in practice, unto yesterday.

Psalm cxliii. 8 *to* 11.

CAUSE me to hear thy loving kindness in the morning; for in thee do I trust: cause me to know the way wherein I should walk; for I lift up my soul unto thee.

Deliver me, O Lord, from mine enemies; I flee unto thee to hide me.

Teach me to do thy will; for thou art my God: thy Spirit is good; lead me into the land of uprightness.

Quicken me, O Lord, for thy name's sake; for thy righteousness' sake bring my soul out of trouble.

REMOVE from my soul thoughts that are without understanding; (*Wisd.* i. 5.) but inspire me with such as are good, and well-pleasing in thy sight.

Turn away mine eyes from beholding vanity; (*Psalm* cxix. 37.) let mine eyes look right on, and let mine eyelids look straight before me.—*Prov.* iv. 25.

Hedge in mine ears with thorns, that they listen not to foolish discourses: (*Ecclus.* xxviii 24.) waken mine ear to hear in the morning, (*Isa.* l. 4.) that I may hearken to the words of thy teaching.

Set a watch, O Lord, before my mouth; keep the door of my lips.—*Psalm* cxli. 3.

Let my speech be seasoned with salt, (*Col.* iv. 6.) that it may minister grace unto the hearers.—*Eph.* iv. 29.

Let nothing that I shall do be a grief or an offence of heart unto me (1 *Sam.* xxv. 31); but let my doings be such, as that thou mayest remember me for good concerning them, and spare me according to the greatness of thy mercy.—*Neh.* xiii. 31. 22.

INTO thy hands I commit my spirit, my soul, my body; thou hast created, redeemed, and regenerated them, O Lord God of truth.—*Ps.* xxxi. 5.

And, with myself, I commend unto thee all those whom I love, and all that which I possess; thou, O Lord, hast graciously given them to me.—*Gen.* xxxiii. 5.

Preserve us from all evil, preserve our souls, O Lord, I beseech thee.—*Psalm* cxxi. 7.

Keep us from falling, and present us faultless before the presence of thy glory (*Jude* 24.) in that day.—2 *Tim.* i. 18.

PRESERVE my going out, and my coming in, from this time forth, and even for evermore.—*Psalm* cxxi. 8.

Prosper thy servant this day, and grant him favour in the sight of all who shall converse with him.—*Neh.* i. 11.

Make haste, O God, to deliver me; make haste, O Lord, to help me.—*Psalm* lxx. 1.

O turn unto me, and have mercy upon me; give thy strength unto thy servant, and save the son of thine handmaid:

Show me a token for good, that I be not put to shame in the sight of them which hate me; because thou, Lord, hast holpen me, and comforted me.—*Psalm* lxxxvi. 16, 17.

SUNDAY.

THROUGH the tender mercy of our God, the dayspring from on high hath visited us.—*Luke* i. 78.

Glory be to thee, O Lord, glory be to thee, who, as on this day, didst create the light, and enlighten the world; (*Gen.* i. 3.)

    The visible light;

    The rays of the sun, the flame of fire, the day and the night, the evening and the morning. —*Gen.* i. 5.

    The intellectual light;

That which is known of God,—*Rom.* i. 19.

That which is written in the law.—*Luke* x. 26.

    The revelations of Prophets,

    The melody of Psalms,

    The instruction of Proverbs,

    The experience of Histories.

A light which hath no evening.

GOD is the Lord, which hath shewed us light; keep holiday in multitudes, even unto the horns of the altar.—*Psalm* cxviii. 27.

By thy resurrection, raise us up unto newness of life (*Rom.* vi. 4.); grafting in us fruits meet for repentance.—*Matt.* iii. 8.

Now the God of peace, that brought again from the dead our Lord Jesus Christ, that great Shepherd of the sheep, through the blood of the everlasting covenant;

Make us perfect in every good work to do his will, working in us that which is well-pleasing in his sight, through Jesus Christ; to whom be glory for ever and ever.—*Heb.* xiii. 20, 21.

O THOU who, on this day, didst send down thy most holy Spirit on thy disciples, take not, O Lord, that holy Spirit from us, (*Ps.* li. 11.) but daily renew it in us who call upon thee.—*Chrysost. Lit.*

AN ACT OF CONFESSION.

MERCIFUL and gracious Lord, long-suffering, and of great goodness; (*Exod.* xxxiv. 6.) I have sinned, O Lord, I have sinned against thee.

O wretched man that I am! (*Rom.* vii. 24.) I have sinned against thee, O, Lord; many times and grievously I have sinned; and that by observing vanities and lies.—*Jonah* ii. 8.

I hide nothing from thee; I pretend no vain excuses.

I give thee glory, O Lord, this day; I make confession of my sins against myself:

Indeed I have sinned against the Lord; and thus, and thus I have done.—*Josh.* vii. 19, 20.

O, what have I done!—*Jer.* viii. 6.

Yet he hath not rewarded me according to my iniquities.—*Psalm* ciii. 10.

And now, what shall I say? or how shall I open my mouth? what shall I answer? for I, even I, have done it. I am without excuse, without defence;—*Rom.* ii. 1.

Condemned of my own judgment:- *Tit.* iii. 11.

My destruction cometh of myself.—*Hos.* xiii. 9.

O Lord, righteousness belongeth unto thee, but unto me confusion of face.—*Dan.* ix. 7.

Howbeit, thou art just in all that is brought upon me; for thou hast done right, but I have done wickedly.—*Neh.* ix. 33.

And now, Lord, what wait I for? Is it not for thee? Even so: my hope is in thee;—*Psalm* xxxix. 7.

If haply I have hope left me of deliverance; if thy loving-kindness may surpass the multitude of my offences.

Remember how short my time is. — *Psalm* lxxxix. 47.

Remember that I am the work of thy hands.—*Psalm* cxxxviii. 8.

> The image of thy countenance.—*Gen.* i. 26.
> The price of thy blood.—1 *Cor.* vi. 20.
> An heir of thy name.—*Acts* xi. 26.
> A sheep of thy pasture.—*Psalm* c. 3.
> A child of thy covenant.—*Acts* iii. 25.

Forsake not the works of thine own hands.—*Psalm* cxxxviii. 8.

Behold thine own image and likeness.—*Gen.* i. 26.

Hast thou made any thing in vain?—*Psalm* lxxxix. 47.

Surely in vain, if thou destroy it.

And what profit is there in my destruction?—*Psalm* xxx. 9.

Thine enemies will rejoice over me.—*Psalm* xxxv. 19.

Let them never rejoice, O Lord.—*Ps.* xxxv. 19.

Let not thine enemies be gratified, when my foot slippeth.—*Psalm* xxxviii. 16.

Look upon the face of thine anointed.—*Psalm* lxxxiv. 9.

And, by the blood of thy covenant,—*Zech.* ix. 11.

By the propitiation of the whole world,—1 *John* ii. 2.

Lord, be merciful to me a sinner;—*Luke* xviii. 13.

Lord, be merciful to me, the first of sinners;

The chief and the greatest of sinners.—1 *Tim.* i. 15.

For thy name's sake also pardon mine iniquity; for it is great (*Psalm* xxv. 11.): assuredly it is very great.

Even for that thy name, beside which there is none other name under heaven given among men, whereby we must be saved:—*Acts* iv. 12.

The Spirit himself helping our infirmity, and making intercession for us with groanings which cannot be uttered.—*Rom.* viii. 26.

For the tender bowels of the Father,

For the bleeding wounds of the Son,

For the unspeakable groans of the Holy Ghost,

O Lord, hear; O Lord, forgive; O Lord, hearken and do; defer not, for thine own sake, O Lord, O Lord my God!—*Dan.* ix. 19.

As for me, I acknowledge my transgressions: my sins are ever before me.—*Psalm* li. 3.

I recount them in the bitterness of my soul: (*Job* vii. 11.) I will be sorry for them.—*Psalm* xxxviii. 18.

I turn myself and groan,
I am moved with indignation,
I take vengeance on myself,
I reproach myself,
I abhor and chasten myself,
Because my affliction is not greater,
Because my sorrow is not more ample.
Lord, I repent; Lord, I repent;
Help thou mine impenitence;
And continually more and more,
Pierce, grieve, and grind my heart.

Pass by, forgive, and pardon all that is a grief unto me, or offendeth my heart.—1 *Sam.* xxv. 31.

Cleanse thou me from secret faults; keep back thy servant also from presumptuous sins.—*Psalm* xix. 12, 13.

Magnify thy mercy towards me, a miserable sinner, and say unto me in due season, O Lord,

Be of good cheer, thy sins be forgiven thee:—*Matt.* ix. 2.

My grace is sufficient for thee.—2 *Cor.* xii. 9.

Say unto my soul, I am thy salvation.—*Psalm* xxxv. 3.

Why art thou cast down, O my soul? and why art thou disquieted within me?—*Psalm* xlii. 11.

Return unto thy rest, O my soul; for the Lord will deal bountifully with thee.—*Psalm* cxvi. 7.

From the Seven Penitential Psalms.

O Lord, rebuke me not in thine anger; neither chasten me in thy displeasure.—*Psalm* vi. 1.

I said, I will confess my transgression unto the Lord; and thou forgavest the iniquity of my heart.—*Psalm* xxxii. 5.

Lord, all my desire is before thee; and my groaning is not hid from thee.—*Psalm* xxxviii. 9.

Have mercy upon me, O God, according to thy great loving-kindness; and according to the multitude of thy mercies blot out my transgressions.—*Psalm* li. 1.

Thou shalt arise, and have mercy upon me, O Lord; for the time to favour me, yea, the set time is come.—*Psalm* cii. 13.

If thou, Lord, shouldst mark iniquities, O Lord, who shall stand?—*Psalm* cxxx. 13.

Enter not into judgment with thy servant; for in thy sight shall no man living be justified.—*Ps.* cxliii. 2.

A PRAYER FOR GRACE.

My hands I lift up unto thy commandments, which I have loved.—*Psalm* cxix. 48.

Open thou mine eyes, and I shall behold.—*Verse* 18.

Incline my heart, and I shall love thee.—*Ver.* 36.

Order my steps, (*Verse* 133.) and I shall go in the path of thy commandments.—*Verse* 35.

O Lord God, be thou my God;
But beside thee let me have none other,
None other, and nothing else but thee.—*Ps.* lxxiii. 25.

Grant that I may worship thee and serve thee,
In spirit and in truth,—*John* iv. 24.
In bodily devoutness and decency,—1 *Cor.* xiv. 40.
With the praises of my tongue,—*Verse* 26.
Publicly as well as privately.

Grant also, that I may render
Honour to those who have rule over me,
By submitting myself to them,
By obeying them:—*Heb.* xiii. 7.
Natural affection to those who belong unto me,
By taking care of them,
By providing for them.—1 *Tim.* v. 8.
Grant that I may overcome evil with good;—*Rom.* xii. 21.
That I may possess my vessel in sanctification and honour;—1 *Thess.* iv. 4.
That I may have my conversation without covetousness, and be content with such things as I have;—*Heb.* xiii. 5.
That I may speak the truth in love;—*Eph.* iv. 15.
That I may desire without concupiscence;—1 *Thess.* iv. 5.
Especially that I add not lasciviousness to concupiscence,—1 *Pet.* iv. 3.
Nor walk after mine own lusts.—*Jude* 16.

THE FENCE OF THE LAW:
RULES OF CAUTION, AND HELPS TO OBEDIENCE.

Give me grace, O Lord,
To bruise the serpent's head;—*Gen.* iii. 15.
To consider my latter end;—*Deut.* xxxii. 29.
To cut off occasions of sin;—2 *Cor.* xi. 12.
To be sober;—1 *Pet.* v. 8.
Not to stand in idleness;—*Matt.* xx. 6.
Not to sit with the wicked;—*Psalm* xxvi. 5.
To cleave unto the good;—*Rom.* xii. 9.
To make a covenant with mine eyes;—*Job* xxxi. 1.
To bring my body into subjection;—1 *Cor.* ix. 27.
To give myself unto prayer;—1 Cor. vii. 5.
To come to repentance.—2 *Pet.* iii. 9.

Hedge up my way with thorns, that I find not the path to follow after vanity.—*Hosea* ii. 6.

Hold in my mouth with bit and bridle, when I come not near unto thee.—*Psalm* xxxii. 9.

O Lord, compel me to come in unto thee.—*Luke* xiv. 23.

AN ACT OF FAITH.

I believe in thee, O Lord,
The Father,
The Word, } One God.—1 *John* v. 7.
The Spirit,

1. That by thy Fatherly mercy and power all things were created.

That by thy goodness and thy love towards man all things are restored.

2. In thy Word:

Who, for us men and for our salvation, was made flesh;

Was conceived, was born,

Suffered and was crucified,

Dead, and buried;

He descended, he rose again,

He ascended, he sat at the right hand;

He shall return, and render unto every man.

3. That, by the illumination and operation of thy Holy Spirit,

A peculiar people is called out of the whole world into one society,—*Tit.* ii. 14.

Unto belief of the truth,—2 *Thess.* ii. 13.

And holiness of conversation:—1 *Pet.* iii. 2.

That, in this Spirit,

We are made partakers

Of the communion of the saints,

Of the remission of sins,

In this life present;

And that, in the same Spirit, we assuredly look for

The resurrection of the flesh, and life everlasting,

In the world to come.

THIS most holy faith,

Once delivered unto the saints,—*Jude* 3.

I believe, O Lord;

Help thou mine unbelief.—*Mark* ix. 24.
Increase my little faith;—*Luke* xvii. 5.

   And mercifully grant
That I may love the Father for his goodness,
And adore the Almighty for his power;
That I may commit the keeping of my soul to him in well-doing, as unto a faithful Creator.—1 *Pet.* iv. 19.

   Grant that I may share
Salvation of Jesus,
Unction of Christ,
Adoption of the only-begotten Son.

   That I may worship the Lord,

For His conception,	In faith;
For His birth,	In humility;
For His sufferings,	In patience, and in hatred of sin;
For His cross,	In crucifying the first emotions of the flesh;—*Gal.* v. 24.
For His death,	In mortifying the flesh;
For His burial,	In burying evil thoughts by good works;
For His descent,	In descending by frequent meditation into hell;
For His resurrection,	In rising up unto newness of life;—*Rom.* vi. 4.
For His ascension,	In setting my affection on things above;—*Col.* iii. 2.
For His sitting at the	In giving unto godliness the

right hand of the Father,	first place in my heart;
For His return from thence,	In awe of His second coming;
For His judgment of the world,	In judging myself, that I be not judged by Him.— 1 *Cor.* xi. 31.

Grant, that I may receive from the Spirit
    The breath of saving grace,
That in the Church I may be partaker of Election,
In the Holy Church, of Sanctification.
In the Catholic Church, of Communication;
    And of a share in
  Its sacraments and prayers,
  Its fastings and groanings,
  Its watchings and tears,
    Its afflictions;
Unto an assurance of the remission of my sins,
Unto a hope of resurrection and translation to eternal life.

O THOU, that art the hope of all the ends of the earth, and of them that remain in the broad sea; —*Ps.* lxv. 5.

O thou, in whom our fathers trusted, and thou didst deliver them; in whom they trusted, and were not confounded;—*Ps.* xxii. 4, 5.

O thou, that hast been my hope from my youth; (*Ps.* lxxi. 5.) even when I was upon my mother's breasts; (*Ps.* xxii. 9.) upon whom I was cast from the womb;—*Verse* 10.

Be thou my refuge henceforth and for ever, and my portion in the land of the living.—*Ps.* cxlii. 5.

My hope is in the goodness of thy nature, in the excellency of thy names, in thy types and figures, in thy word and works:

Let me not be ashamed of my hope.—*Psalm* cxix. 116.

AN ACT OF INTERCESSION.

O THOU who art the confidence of all the ends of the earth, (*Ps.* lxv. 5.) remember every work of thine hand for good, and visit the world in thy mercy.

O thou Preserver of men, (*Job* vii. 20.) O Lord, thou Lover of mankind, think graciously of all our race; and as thou hast included all in unbelief, have mercy upon all, O Lord.—*Rom.* xi. 32.

O thou who to this end didst die and rise again, that thou mightest be Lord both of the dead and living;—*Rom.* xiv. 9.

Whether we live or whether we die, thou art our Lord;—*Verse* 8.

Whether living or dying, have mercy on us, O Lord.

O thou, the helper of the helpless, a seasonable refuge in the time of trouble;—*Psalm* ix. 9.

Remember all who lie under sad necessity, and stand in need of thy protection.

O thou, the God of grace and truth,—*John* i. 14.

Establish all who stand in thy truth and grace;—2 *Pet.* i. 12.

Restore all who labour under heresy or sin.—*Gal.* vi. 1.

O thou, the Protector of thy Christ's anointed, remember thy congregation which thou hast purchased and redeemed of old:—*Psalm* lxxiv. 2.

O, let them that believe be of one heart and of one soul.—*Acts* iv. 32.

O thou, who walkest in the midst of the golden candlesticks,—*Rev.* ii. 1.

Remove not this our candlestick out of his place.—*Verse* 5.

Set in order the things that are wanting;—*Tit.* i. 5.

Strengthen the things which thou wouldst reject, that are ready to die.—*Rev.* iii. 2.

O thou, the Lord of the harvest, send forth labourers sufficiently enabled by thee to do the work of thy harvest.—*Matt.* ix. 38.

O thou, who art the portion of them (*Ps.* cxix. 57.) who minister about thy temple,—1 *Cor.* ix. 13.

Grant unto thy clergy that they may rightly divide the word of truth, (2 *Tim.* ii. 15.) and walk uprightly in the same:—*Gal.* ii. 14.

Grant that unto them the beloved of Christ may submit themselves, and obey them.—*Heb.* xiii. 17.

O thou, the King of nations even to the ends of

the earth, strengthen all the kingdoms and governments of the whole earth; for they are thy ordinance, (*Rom.* xiii. 2.) albeit an institution of man. —1 *Pet.* ii. 13.

Scatter thou the people that delight in war;— *Psalm* lxviii. 30.

Make wars to cease in all the world.—*Psalm* xlvi. 9.

O Lord, upon whom the isles do wait and trust, —*Isaiah* li. 5.

Deliver this island, and the whole country wherein we dwell, from all affliction, peril, and necessity.—*Lit. Chrys.*

O Lord of lords, and King of kings, be mindful of all princes, whom thou hast deputed to rule on earth.

And especially be mindful of our gracious king, thy servant; assist him more and more, and prosper him in all things; suggest good counsels unto his heart, for thy church and for thy people's sake; grant and continue unto him profound peace, that we, partaking of his tranquillity, may lead a quiet and peaceable life in all godliness and honesty.— 1 *Tim.* ii. 2.

O thou, by whom powers are ordained,—*Rom.* xiii. 1.

Grant unto all that be in eminency at the court, that they be also eminent in virtue and in fear of thee.

Grant unto the council thy godly wisdom;

To our nobles, that they be able to do nothing against the truth, but for the truth;—2 *Cor.* xiii. 8.

To our judges, a respect for thy judgment, and that they judge all men in all things without preferring one before another, doing nothing by partiality.—1 *Tim.* v. 21.

O God of Sabaoth, God of Hosts,

Guide and protect all Christian armies against the enemies of our most holy faith.

Grant unto our whole nation to be subject unto the higher powers, (*Rom.* xiii. 1.) not only for wrath, but also for conscience' sake.—*Verse 5.*

Grant to our husbandmen and herdsmen seasons of fertility;

To our merchants and fishermen, successful voyages;

To our tradesmen, honesty and contentment;

To our artificers, even to the poorest mechanic, and to the beggar, the will to follow their respective labours with diligence and patience.

O God, the God not of ourselves alone, but also of our posterity; bless our children among us, that they may increase, as in stature, so in wisdom, and in favour with thee and man.—*Luke* ii. 52.

Thou who desirest us to provide for our own, (1 *Tim.* v. 8.) and hatest them that are without natural affection;—2 *Tim.* iii. 3.

Be mindful, O Lord, of my kinsmen according to the flesh; (*Romans* ix. 3.) and give me grace to speak peace of them, and to seek after their good.

Thou that desirest us to recompense our benefactors, remember for good, O Lord, all those who have dealt kindly by me; preserve them, and make them blessed upon the earth, and deliver them not unto the will of their enemies.—*Psalm* xli. 2.

Thou who hast denounced that man, who provideth not for his own household, to be worse than an infidel;—1 *Tim.* v. 8.

Be mindful, according to thy good pleasure, of all my family;

Peace be to my house; the Son of peace be on all within it.—*Luke* x. 5, 6.

Thou that desirest our righteousness should exceed the righteousness of sinners;—*Matt.* v. 20.

Grant, O Lord, that I may love them which love me;—*Verse* 46.

That I may never forsake mine own friends, nor my father's friends, nor the children of my friends. —*Prov.* xxvii. 10.

Thou who hast commanded us to overcome evil with good, (*Rom.* xii. 21.) and to pray for them which despitefully use us, and persecute us;—*Matt.* v. 44.

Be merciful to my enemies, O Lord, even as to myself, and bring them, with me also, into thy heavenly kingdom.

Thou who regardest the intercessions which thy servants prefer for one another, remember for **good**,

O Lord, and show mercy unto all, who remember me in their prayers, and unto all whom I have promised to remember in mine.

Thou who in every good work acceptest of a willing mind;—*2 Cor.* viii. 12.

Be mindful of those, O Lord, who, from reasonable hindrances, have no opportunities for prayer, even as of those who pray.

THOU shalt arise and have mercy upon them that are in extremity; for the time to favour them, yea the set time is come.—*Psalm* cii. 13.

Be merciful unto them, O Lord, even as unto myself in my extremities.

Be mindful, O Lord, of our
    Infants, children, youths,
        With those of riper manhood,
        And those declining into old age.
            Be mindful of
    The hungry and thirsty,
    The naked and sick,
    The prisoner and the stranger,
    The houseless and the unburied.

Of those whom years have rendered impotent;

Of those whom the devil hath importuned to destroy themselves;

Of those which are vexed with unclean spirits; —*Acts* v. 16.

Of those who have sunk into despair;

Of the diseased in mind or body;

Of the faint-hearted;
Of those who lie in imprisonment or bonds;
Of those condemned to die.
   Be mindful
Of all orphans and widows;
Of those who travel by land or by water;
Of women labouring with child, or giving suck;
Of the slave to a hard task-master;
Of the labourer in the mines or at the galleys;
Of the wanderer in desert places.

PRESERVE, O Lord, both man and beast.

How excellent is thy loving-kindness, O God! therefore the children of men shall put their trust under the shadow of thy wings.—*Ps.* xxxvi. 6, 7.

The Lord bless us, and keep us; the Lord make his face shine upon us, and be gracious unto us; the Lord lift up his countenance upon us, and give us peace.—*Numb.* vi. 24, 25, 26.

UNTO thee, O Lord, I commend
 My soul and body,
 My mind and thoughts,
 My prayers and all my wishes,
 My senses and limbs,
 My life and my death;
My brothers and sisters, and their children;
My friends, benefactors, and intercessors;
My friends and neighbours;
My country, and all Christian people.

AN ACT OF PRAISE.

Let us lift up our hearts unto the Lord :—*Liturg.*

As it is very meet, and right, our proper and bounden duty, that we should by all means and on all occasions, in every place, and time, and mode, ever, every where, and every way,

 Remember Thee, confess unto Thee,
 Bless Thee, worship Thee;
 Praise Thee, celebrate Thee;
  Give thanks unto Thee;

The
- Creator and Nourisher
- Preserver, Governor, and Keeper
- Beginner and Finisher
- Lord and Father
- King and God

of all men;

The fountain of life and immortality;
The treasury of eternal bliss,
 Whom the heavens do praise,
  And heavens of heavens;
The angels, and all the powers of heaven,
Continually crying among themselves,
(And we, base and unworthy, with them, at their feet,)

  Holy, holy, holy,
  Lord God of Hosts!

The whole heavens and the whole earth are full of thy majesty and glory.—*Isai.* vi. 3.

BLESSED be the glory of the Lord from his place,
—*Ezek.* iii. 12.

For His
- Godhead,
- Incomprehensibility,
- Sublimity,
- Dominion,
- Omnipotence,
- Eternity,
- Providence.

The Lord is my
- Strength and rock,
- Fortress and deliverer,
- Helper and defender,

The horn of my salvation,
And my high tower.—*Ps.* xviii. 1, 2.

MONDAY.

My voice shalt thou hear in the morning, O Lord; in the morning will I stand before thee, and thou shalt see me.—*Psalm* v. 3.

Blessed art thou, O Lord, who, as on this day, didst create the firmament of heaven, (*Gen.* i. 6.) the heavens, and heavens of heavens, the celestial powers, angels, archangels, cherubim and seraphim:

1. The waters above the firmament;—*Gen.* i. 7.

    Mists and exhalations,

        From whence proceed

    Clouds from the ends of the earth,—*Psalm* cxxxv. 7.

    Dew, showers, and hail;

    Snow like wool,

    Hoar-frost like ashes,

    And ice like morsels;—*Psalm* cxlvii. 16, 17.

    Thunders and lightnings,—*Rev.* xvi. 18.

    Winds and tempests out of his treasures.—*Ps.* cxxxv. 7.

2. The waters under the firmament,—*Gen.* i. 7.

    For refreshment,

    For purification.

AN ACT OF CONFESSION.

I will confess mine iniquities, and the iniquities of my fathers; for I have dealt corruptly against thee, and neglected thee, O Lord, and walked contrary to thy commandments.—*Ps.* xxxii. 5. *Neh.* i. 6, 7. *Levit.* xxvi. 40.

Set not, O Lord, set not mine iniquities before thee; my way of life in the light of thy countenance:—*Psalm* xc. 8.

But pardon the iniquity of thy servant according unto the greatness of thy mercy, and as thou hast forgiven me from childhood even until now.—*Numb.* xiv. 19.

I have sinned; what shall I do unto thee, O thou Preserver of men? Why hast thou set me as a mark against thee, so that I am a burden to myself?—*Job* vii. 20.

Hide thy face from my sins, and blot out all mine iniquity.—*Psalm* li. 9.

Deliver my soul from going down to the pit; for thou hast found a ransom.—*Job* xxxiii. 24.

Have mercy on me, thou Son of David!—*Matt.* xv. 22.

Lord, help me!—*Verse* 25.

Yea, Lord; for even the dogs eat of the crumbs which fall from their masters' table.—*Verse* 27.

Lord, have patience with me;—*Matt.* xviii. 26.

Nay, rather, I have not wherewith to pay;—
Verse 25.

I will confess unto thee:

Forgive me the whole debt, I beseech thee.—
Verse 27.

How long wilt thou forget me, O Lord? How ong wilt thou hide thy face from me?—*Psalm* xiii. 1.

How long shall I take counsel in my soul, having sorrow in my heart by day and night? How long shall mine enemy be exalted over me?—*Verse* 2.

Consider and hear me, O Lord my God; lighten mine eyes, lest I sleep the sleep of death:—*Ver.* 3.

Lest mine enemy say, I have prevailed against him; and those that trouble me rejoice when I am moved.—*Verse* 4.

But I have trusted in thy mercy.—*Verse* 5.

A PRAYER FOR GRACE TO KEEP THE COMMANDMENTS.

REMOVE from me, O Lord,
  I. All impiety and profaneness,
     All superstition and hypocrisy.
 II. Idolatry and self-worship.
III. Rash oaths and cursing.
 IV. Withdrawment from thy public worship, or irreverent attendance.
  V. Disobedience and neglect.
 VI. Contention and wrath.
VII. Lust and uncleanness.
VIII. Idleness and dishonesty.
 IX. Falsehood and slander.
  X. Every depraved thought; every impure imagination; every base desire; every unbeseeming wish.

IMPART unto me
  I. Piety and devotion.
 II. Adoration and worship.

III. The language of blessing, and a religious observance of my oath.
IV. Decency and humility in thy public congregation.
V. Natural affection and deference.
VI. Long-suffering and gentleness.
VII. Chastity and temperance.
VIII. Contentedness and honesty.
IX. Truth and integrity.
X. Good thoughts, and perseverance to the end.

THE APOSTLES' CREED.

I BELIEVE IN GOD:—

I. THE FATHER ALMIGHTY, Maker of Heaven and Earth.
II. JESUS CHRIST, His only Son, our Lord;
Who 1. Was conceived by the Holy Ghost.
    2. Born of the Virgin Mary.
    3. Suffered under Pontius Pilate.
    4. Was crucified.
    5. Died.
    6. Was buried.
    7. Descended into hell.
    8. Rose again from the dead.
    9. Ascended into heaven.
    10. Sitteth at the right hand of the Father.
    11. Will come again from thence,
    12. To judge the quick and the dead.
III. THE HOLY GHOST.
    1. The Holy Church.

2. The Catholic.
3. The communion of saints.
4. The forgiveness of sins.
5. The resurrection of the flesh.
6. Everlasting life.

AND now, what is my hope?
Art not thou, O Lord?—*Psalm* xxxix. 8.
O Lord, in thee have I trusted: let me not be confounded for ever.—*Te Deum.*

AN ACT OF INTERCESSION.

LET us pray to God,
In behalf of all his creatures,
 To grant us seasons of health, fertility, and peace.
In behalf of the whole human race:
 1. For such as be not Christians;
That Atheists
  Blasphemers
  Heathens   } may be converted.
  Turks and
  Jews
 2. For Christians;
That those who labour under sin and error may be restored;
That those who are by thee endowed with truth and grace may be confirmed.
Let us pray for help and consolation unto all
 Who are diseased in mind or body.

For all and every one,
  Both male and female,
Who may be straitened in poverty or want.
For thankfulness and humility on their parts,

Who enjoy
- Cheerfulness of mind.
- Health of body.
- Affluence in estate.
- Expedience in counsel.

For the universal Church;
  That it be strengthened and enlarged.
For the Eastern Church;
  That it be freed and united.
For the Western Church;
  That it be re-established in peace.
For the Church of England;
  That its deficiencies be supplied,
  Its present prosperity secured to it.
Let us pray for the bishops and clergy,
  And for all Christian people.
  For all estates throughout the world;
    Those of Christianity though far away;
    Those which border on our own;
    This, to which we ourselves pertain.
  For all in authority;
    Our king, by the grace of God preserved to us;
    Our queen and prince;
    The officers of state,
    Privy-council, judges, soldiery, and magistrates;

The people, with their respective officers;
Husbandmen, herdsmen, and fishermen;
Merchants, tradesmen, and mechanics;
Even to the poor labourer and the beggar.
For the increase and sound education
 Of all the royal family,
 And the children of our nobles,
 In our { Universities, Inns of court, Schools, both of town and country,
and in every branch of art and science.
For all who are commended to my prayers
 By kindred or alliance;
  For my brothers and sisters,
  That God's blessing may be on them
  And on their children.
 By the obligation of benefits received;
That God may requite all who have ministered
 The necessaries of this life unto me.
  By charge entrusted to my care;
For all who have at any time been
 Instructed or ordained by me.
For my College; for my Parish.
For the Collegiate Church of Southwell.
For the Cathedral of St. Paul.
For the Abbey of Westminster.
 For the Dioceses of { Chichester, Ely, } which I once held.
For that of Winchester, which I now retain.
 And therein for the clergy and laity,

The priests and deacons.
For the deanery of the Chapel Royal.
For the dispensership of the king's alms.
For the colleges committed to my visitation.
 By moral friendship;
For those who wish me well,
 Though some of them unknown to me.
 By Christian charity;
For those that hate me without a cause,
And some even for truth and righteousness' sake.
 By vicinity of situation;
For those who dwell near me
 In quietness and peace.
  By promise;
For all whom I have pledged myself to remember
 In my prayers.
  By mutual duty.
For all who remember me in their prayers,
 And require a like return of me.
For those who on reasonable grounds
But rarely attend thy public worship,
 As oppressed and hurried
  By weight of business.
For those who have no one especially
 To intercede for them.
For those who are at this time warring
 Against extreme necessity,
  And with unequal prowess.
For those who are bent on any signal undertaking,

By which the glory of God's name,
Or the real welfare of his Church
    May be promoted.
For those who have shewn charity
    Towards the Church or the poor.
For all who have at any time been brought to reproach
    By my word or deed.

GOD be merciful unto me, and bless me; and shew me the light of his countenance, and be merciful unto me.—*Psalm* lxvii. 1.
    God give me his blessing;—*Verse* 6.
    The Lord receive my prayer.—*Psalm* vi. 9.
    Direct my life, O God, after thy commandments;
    Sanctify my soul;
    Purify my body;
    Rectify my thoughts;
    Cleanse my appetites:
      My soul and body,
      My mind and spirit,
      My heart and my reins;—*Psalm* vii. 9.
    Lord, make me clean altogether;
      For, if thou wilt, thou canst.—*Luke* v. 12.

AN ACT OF PRAISE.

THE Lord, he is the Lord God,
    Merciful and gracious,
    Long-suffering,

And abundant in goodness and truth:
Who keepeth mercy for thousands,
Who forgiveth iniquity,
And transgressions, and sins,
And will by no means clear the guilty.
Who visiteth the iniquity of the fathers
Upon the children.—*Exod.* xxxiv. 6, 7.
I will bless the Lord at all times:
> His praise shall continually be in my mouth.
> —*Psalm* xxxiv. 1.

GLORY to GOD in the HIGHEST,
> On earth peace,
> Good will toward men!—*Luke* ii. 14.

The Hierarchy of Heavenly Essences, commonly called The Nine Orders of Angels, with their distinct Operations.

Angels,	Tuition.
Archangels, 1 *Thess.* iv. 16.	Illumination.
Virtues, 1 *Pet.* ii. 9.	Miracles.
Thrones,	Judgment;
Dominions,	Beneficence;
Principalities,	Government;
Powers, *Col.* i. 16.	The subversion of Devils.
Cherubim, *Gen.* iii. 24.	Knowledge.
Seraphim, *Isaiah* vi. 6.	Charity.

TUESDAY.

O God, thou art my God; early will I seek thee.—*Psalm* lxiii. 1.

Blessed art thou, O Lord, who, as on this day, didst gather together the waters into the sea, and lettest the dry land appear.—*Gen.* i. 9.

Who didst also bring forth the seed of grass, and of the tree yielding fruit after his kind.—*Verse* 11.

Lo! the depths and seas, as in a bottle;—*Job* xxxviii. 37.

The lakes, rivers, and fountains;
The earth; the continent and islands;
The mountains, hills, and vallies;
The fields, the meadows, and the lawns:
Green grass, and corn, and hay:
 Herbs and flowers,
For food, luxury, and medicine;
 Trees yielding fruit;
Fruit for wine, oil, and spices;
 Things under the earth, for the use of man,
 Metals and minerals,
 Stones and coals:
Blood, and fire, and vapour of smoke.—*Joel* ii. 30.

AN ACT OF CONFESSION.

Who can understand his errors? Cleanse thou me from secret faults.—*Psalm* xix. 12.

Keep back thy servant also from presumptuous sins; let them not have dominion over me.—*Ver.* 13.

For thy name's sake, O Lord, pardon mine iniquity; for it is great.—*Psalm* xxv. 11.

Mine iniquities have taken hold upon me, so that I am not able to look up; they are more in number than the hairs of mine head, therefore my heart faileth me.—*Psalm* xl. 12.

Be pleased, O Lord, to deliver me; O Lord, make haste to help me.—*Verse* 13.

Shew thy marvellous loving-kindness unto me, O thou that savest them which put their trust in thee.—*Psalm* xvii. 7.

I said, Lord, be merciful unto me; heal my soul, for I have sinned against thee.—*Psalm* xli. 4.

I have sinned, but I am ashamed, and turn from my wicked ways, and bethink myself of mine own heart, and with all my heart return to thee, and seek thy face, and entreat thee, saying:

I have sinned, I have done amiss, I have dealt wickedly; I know, O Lord, the pollution of my heart, and lo! I return to thee with all my heart and with all my strength.—2 *Chron.* vi. 37, 38.

And now hear thou, O Lord, from thy dwelling-place, and from the throne of the glory of thy kingdom in Heaven, the prayer and supplications of thy servant.—*Verse* 39.

O Lord, be reconciled unto thy servant, and heal his soul.—*Psalm* xli. 4.

God, be merciful to me a sinner;—*Luke* xviii. 13.

Be merciful to me, the chief of sinners.—1 *Tim.* i. 15.

Father, I have sinned against heaven, and before thee, and am no more worthy to be called thy son: make me as one of thy hired servants;—*Luke* xv. 18, 19.

Make me one, though the last and lowest of them all.

What profit is there in my blood, when I go down to the pit? Shall the dust praise thee? shall it confess thy truth?—*Psalm* xxx. 9.

Hear, O Lord, and have mercy upon me; Lord, be thou my helper.—*Verse* 10.

Turn my heaviness into joy.—*Verse* 11.

A PRAYER FOR GRACE.

Turn, O Lord, I beseech thee,
 My levity into carefulness,
 My listlessness into self-defence,
 My conscious error into indignation,
 My sin into godly fear,
 My transgression into vehement desire,
 My iniquity into zeal,
 My abomination into revenge!—2 *Cor.* vii. 11.

AN ACT OF FAITH.

FAITH.

 1. The Deity:—
  Love, power, providence.

II. Salvation, unction, adoption,
    The Lord's body :—
  His conception, birth, and passion,
    Cross, death, and burial,
    Descent, resurrection, ascension,
    Session, return, judgment.
III. Inspiration and sanctification :—
  Calling out of ⎫
  Sanctifying in ⎬ the world.
  Communion of saints and sanctities,
  Forgiveness of sins,
  Resurrection from the dead,
  Life everlasting.

AN ACT OF INTERCESSION.

BE thou my hope, thou who art the confidence of all the ends of the earth, and of them that are afar off upon the sea.—*Psalm* lxv. 5.

  Protect and bless, O Lord,
    The universe,
    Mankind,
    All who are afflicted or distressed.
      The Church,
    The holy Catholic,
    The Eastern, the Western,
    The church of England.
    All bishops, priests, and deacons,
    All Christian people.
    All estates throughout the world,
    Those converted to Christianity,

Those we may call our neighbours,
This, our own.
All rulers and kings,
Godly men,
Especially our own.
All counsellors, judges, and magistrates;
Soldiers, by sea and land,
The commonalty.
Our offspring,
Our seats of education.
The constituents of the court,
The city, and the country.
Those who minister to our souls or bodies
Food, raiment, medicine,
The necessaries of this life.
Those to whom I am bound
By nature, by obligation,
By trust committed to me
   Now or formerly:
By friendship, charity, neighbourhood,
A promise,
Mutual duty.
All who find no leisure to pray.
The destitute,
The dying.

THE Lord be my keeper, the Lord be my defence upon my right hand.—*Psalm* cxxi. 5.

   The Lord preserve me from all evil; the Lord keep my soul.—*Verse 7.*

The Lord preserve my going out and my coming in, from this time forth for evermore.—*Ver.* 8.

O LORD, thou knowest how, and thou art able and willing, to do good unto my soul.

I, wretched man that I am, (*Rom.* vii. 24.) neither know how, nor am able, nor willing as I ought to be.

Do thou, O Lord, I beseech thee according to thine unspeakable loving-kindness, so order and dispose of me, as thou knowest to be most agreeable unto thee, and most profitable unto me.

THE ATTRIBUTES OF MERCY.

GOODNESS;—2 *Sam.* vii. 28.
  Grace;—*Nehem.* ix. 31.
  Charity;—*Rom.* v. 20.
  Kindness and love;—*Tit.* iii. 4.
  Meekness and gentleness;—2 *Cor.* x. 1.
  Forbearance and long-suffering;—*Rom.* ii. 4.
  Abundant mercy;—1 *Pet.* i. 3.
  Great mercy;—*Psalm* li. 1.
  Compassion;—*Rom.* xii. 1.
  Multitude of compassions;—*Psalm* li. 1.
  Bowels of compassion;—*Col.* iii. 12.
  Tender, most tender, bowels:—*James* v. 11.
In passing by;—*Micah* vii. 18.
In winking and overlooking;—*Acts* xvii. 30.
In holding his peace:—*Isa.* lvii. 11.
    For many times;—*Neh.* ix. 28.

For many years:—*Verse* 30.

Not willingly afflicting, nor from his heart;—*Lament.* iii. 33.

Not letting loose his anger;—*Ps.* lxxviii. 38.

Not according to our iniquities;—*Ps.* ciii. 10.

Not always;—*Verse* 9.

In wrath remembering mercy;—*Hab.* iii. 2.

Repenting him of the evil;—*Joel* ii. 13.

Deeming all his chastisements double;—*Isaiah* xl. 2.

Prone to pardon, to reconcilement, and to propitiation.

WEDNESDAY.

In the morning-watches I will meditate on thee, O Lord; because thou hast been my helper.—*Psalm* lxiii. 6, 7.

Blessed art thou, O Lord, who, as on this day, didst make two lights, the greater light, the sun, and the lesser light, the moon; and the stars also; —*Gen.* i. 16.

To give light upon the earth,—*Verse* 17.

And for signs and for seasons;—*Verse* 14.

For spring, summer, autumn, winter;

For days, weeks, months, and years;

And to rule over the day, and over the night.—*Verse* 18.

AN ACT OF CONFESSION.

Behold, thou art wroth; for we have sinned.—*Isaiah* lxiv. 5.

We are all become as an unclean thing, and all our righteousnesses are as filthy rags; and we all do fade as a leaf, and our iniquities, like the wind, have taken us away.—*Verse* 6.

And now, O Lord, thou art our father; we are the clay; we are all the work of thy hand.—*Verse* 8.

Be not wroth with us very sore, neither remember our iniquity for ever; behold, see, O Lord! we are all thy people.—*Verse* 9.

O Lord, though our iniquities testify against

us, be merciful unto us for thy name's sake; for our backslidings are many, with which we have sinned against thee.—*Jer.* xiv. 7.

Yet thou, O Lord, art in the midst of us, and we are called by thy name; leave us not.—*Ver.* 9.

O Lord, our hope and Saviour in time of trouble, why art thou become as a stranger in thy land, as a wayfaring man that turneth aside to tarry, and as a man astonied, as a mighty man that cannot save?—*Verses* 8, 9.

Lord, forgive our iniquity, and remember our sins no more.—*Jer.* xxxi. 34.

Lord, I am carnal, sold under sin.—*Rom.* vii. 14.

I know that in me (that is, in my flesh) dwelleth no good thing;—*Verse* 18.

For the good that I would, I do not, but the evil which I would not, that I do.—*Verse* 19.

I consent unto thy law, and delight in it, according to the inward man;—*Verses* 16, 22.

But I see another law in my members, warring against the law of my mind, and bringing me into captivity to the law of sin.—*Verse* 23.

O, wretched man that I am! who shall deliver me from the body of this death?—*Verse* 24.

I thank God, through Jesus Christ our Lord, (*Verse* 25.) that where sin abounded, grace did there much more abound.—*Rom.* v. 20.

Thy goodness, O God, leadeth me to repentance.—*Rom.* ii. 4.

O, give me peradventure repentance to recover myself out of the snare of the devil, by whom I am taken captive at his will.—*2 Tim.* ii. 25, 26.

May the time past of my life suffice me to have wrought the will of the flesh; when I walked in concupiscence, in revellings, and banquettings, and every excess of riot.—1 *Pet.* iv. 3, 4.

But thou, O Lamb, without blemish and without spot, who hast redeemed me with thy precious blood;—1 *Pet.* i. 18, 19.

Pity me, by that thy blood, and save me; by that thy blood, and that thy name, beside which there is none other name under heaven given among men, whereby we must be saved.—*Acts* iv. 12.

O God, thou knowest my foolishness, and my sins are not hid from thee.—*Psalm* lxix. 5.

Lord, all my desire is before thee, and my groaning is not hid from thee.—*Psalm* xxxviii. 9.

Let not them that wait on thee, O Lord God of Hosts, be ashamed for my sake; let not those that seek thee be confounded for my sake, O God of Israel.—*Psalm* lxix. 6.

Deliver me out of the mire, and let me not sink; let me be delivered from them that hate me, and out of the deep waters.—*Verse* 14.

Let not the water-flood overflow me, neither let the deep swallow me up, and let not the pit shut her mouth upon me.—*Verse* 15.

The Seven Deadly Sins of the Accursed Nations.—*Deut.* vii. 1.

PRESERVE me, O God,
From the pride of the Amorite,
 the envy of the Hittite,
 the wrath of the Perizzite,
 the gluttony of the Girgashite,
 the wantonness of the Hivite,
 the covetousness of the Canaanite,
And the lukewarmness of the Jebusite.
  And grant me, in their stead,
  Humility and charity,
  Patience and temperance,
  Chastity and contentedness,
   With spiritual zeal.

AN ACT OF FAITH.

I BELIEVE and acknowledge,
In THE FATHER, his paternal affection;
In the Almighty, his saving power;
In the Creator, his providence,
 Whereby the world
Is preserved, governed, and perfected.

In JESUS, his salvation;
In CHRIST, his holy unction;
In the only Son, adoption;

In the Lord, a master's care.

In his conception and nativity,
The purification of our impure conception and nativity.—*Psalm* li. 5.

   In his sufferings, those evils turned away,
     Which we most righteously have deserved.—*Liturgy*.

In his cross, the curse of the law,—*Gal.* iii. 10.
In his death, the sting of death,—1 *Cor.* xv. 56.
In his burial, our final corruption in the grave, } abolished.

In his descent, that we are saved from going whither we merit to go;

In his resurrection, the first-fruits offered of them that sleep;—1 *Cor.* xv. 20.

In his ascension, that he goeth to prepare a place for us;—*John* xiv. 2.

In his seat at the right hand, his willingness to make intercession for us;—*Heb.* vii. 25.

In his second coming, his reception of his own to himself;—*John* xiv. 3.

In his judgment, the reward of every man according to his works.—*Matt.* xvi. 27.

In THE HOLY GHOST, his power from on high,—*Luke* xxiv. 49.

   Secretly and invisibly,
   Yet effectually and undeniably,

Converting unto holiness.

In the Church, the mystical body of those, who are called from all the quarters of the world unto a brotherhood in faith and godliness.

In the Communion of Saints, the mutual participation in sanctification vouchsafed to every member of that mystical body, unto an assurance of the remission of sins, and unto a hope of resurrection from the dead, and of exaltation unto life eternal.

I TRUST in thy mercy, O God, for ever and ever.—*Psalm* lii. 8.

How excellent is thy loving-kindness, O God.—*Psalm* xxxvi. 7.

If I have any hope, it is in thy mercy: let me not be ashamed of this my hope.—*Ps.* cxix. 116.

AN ACT OF INTERCESSION.

WE further call upon thee:
Remember every one, O Lord, for good;—*Nehem.* xiii. 31.
Have mercy upon us all, O Lord,
  Be reconciled unto all.
Give peace unto the multitude of thy people;
Remove offences;
Make wars to cease;—*Psalm* xlvi. 9.
Repress the innovations of heresy.
O God our Saviour, who art the confidence of all the ends of the earth,—*Psalm* lxv. 5.

Grant us thy peace and love.

Be mindful to crown the year with thy goodness;—*Psalm* lxv. 11.

For the eyes of all wait upon thee, and thou givest them their meat in due season;—*Psalm* cxlv. 15.

Thou openest thine hand, and fillest every living thing with thy goodness.—*Psalm* civ. 27, 28. *Psalm* cxlv. 16.

Be mindful of thy holy church, from the one end of the earth unto the other; grant it thy peace, for thou hast purchased it with thy precious blood, (*Acts* xx. 28.) and so establish it even unto the end of the world.

Be mindful of those who bring forth fruit and do good works in thy holy churches; and those who are mindful of the poor and needy, repay thou with thy rich and heavenly gifts: give them,

For earthly things, the blessings of heaven;

For corruptible, those that fade not;

For temporal, those that endure for ever.

Be mindful of those who devote their lives

To virginity, abstinence,

And religious seclusion;

As of those also, who dwell together

In honourable wedlock

Under thy godly fear.

Be mindful of every Christian soul

Under affliction, oppression, or tribulation,

And consequently in need of thy mercy and assistance;

Of our brethren also who are
   In captivity or in prison,
   In bonds or bitter servitude;
Granting to the wanderer a safe return,
   Health to the sick,
   And freedom to the slave.
Be mindful of all pious and faithful princes,
Whom thou hast ordained to rule over the earth.
And especially be mindful, O Lord,
   Of our king, thy servant;
   Strengthen his empire,
   Subdue to him all his enemies,
   Speak to his heart such good things
   As shall be profitable to thy church and people:
   Grant him profound and uninterrupted peace,
   That, under his happy government,
   We may lead a quiet and peaceable life
   In all godliness and honesty.—1 *Tim.* ii. 2.

BE mindful, O Lord,
   Of all principalities and powers;
   Of our brethren in the state,
   Of our leaders in the council and on the bench,
      And of all who fight thy battles for us
         By land or sea.
Furthermore, be pleased to remember, O Lord,
   Our spiritual fathers,
   The venerable order of priests,
   And the whole clergy,

Who rightly divide the word of truth,—2 *Tim.* ii. 15.
And walk uprightly in the same.—*Gal.* ii. 14.

Be mindful, O Lord, of our brethren,
Be mindful of their zeal and devotion,
Who stand around, and join our prayers,
At this sacred hour.
Be mindful of those, also,
Who from causes unavoidable are absent;
Have mercy upon them, as upon us,
According to the multitude of thy mercy.
Fill our garners with all manner of store,—*Psalm* cxliv. 13.
Preserve our families in peace and concord:
Cherish our infants,
Instruct our youth;
Sustain the aged,
Comfort the feeble-minded;—1 *Thess.* v. 14.
Gather the dispersed,
Reclaim the wandering,
And unite them to thy holy, catholic,
And apostolic church.
Release all that are vexed with unclean spirits,
Accompany the voyage of those who sail,
And the journey of those who travel.
Defend the cause of the widows,
And be a father of the fatherless;—*Psalm* lxviii. 5.
Set the captives at liberty,

And heal the sick.
Be mindful of all criminals at the bar,
    Of those in exile, at the mines, and at the galleys;
    Of those in affliction, necessity, and distress;
    And of all who need thy loving-kindness.
Be mindful of those who love us,
    And of those who hate us;
    And of those who charge us, unworthy as we are,
    To remember them in our prayers.
And of all thy people be mindful,
    O Lord our God;
Pour upon all the riches of thy mercy,
    And grant them all things needful unto salvation.
And remember, O God, of thine own accord
    Those whom we have failed to mention,
        Whether through ignorance, or forgetfulness;
        For they are many in number:
But thou knowest the name and condition of each;
    Thou knowest every one from his mother's womb.—*Jer.* i. 5.
Thou, O Lord, art the helper of the helpless,
    The hope of the hopeless;
    The pilot of the tempest-tossed,
    The haven of them who sail,
    The physician of the sick.
    O, make thyself all things unto all men;—
    1 *Cor.* ix. 22.

For thou knowest man and his desire,
His habitation and his wants.
Deliver, O Lord, this city,
And all the country wherein we dwell,
From plague, famine, earthquake, and deluge,
From fire and sword,
From hostile invasion, and civil war.
Appease the schisms of the churches,
Abate the fury of the heathen;
Receive us all into thy kingdom,
Owning us for children of the light;—*Col.* i. 12.
And grant us thy peace and love,
O Lord, our God.
O Lord God, be mindful
Of all spirits and of all flesh,
Which we have named, and which we have not named.
As to us, direct, O Lord,
Direct the period of our lives in peace,
That our death be that of Christians,
Acceptable unto thee,
And, if it be thy pleasure, free from pain.
Gather us together under the feet of thine elect,
When thou wilt, and as thou wilt,
Only without shame and sin.

THE glorious majesty of our Lord be upon us:
Prosper thou the work of our hands upon us,
O, prosper thou our handy-work.—*Psalm* xc. 17.

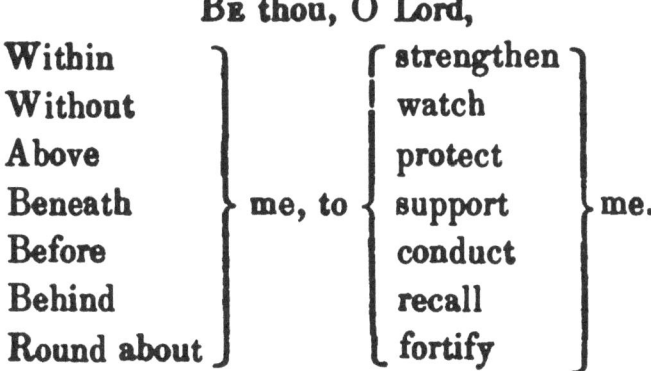

AN ACT OF PRAISE.

Blessed be thou, Lord God of Israel, our Father, for ever and ever.—1 *Chron.* xxix. 10.

Thine, O Lord, is the greatness, and the power, and the glory, and the victory, and the majesty and worship; for all that is in the heaven and in the earth is thine.—*Verse* 11.

Every king of every nation trembleth at thy presence.—*Isai.* lxiv. 2.

Thine is the kingdom, O Lord; and thou art high above all things, and over all dominion.—*Ps.* xcix. 2.

Riches come of thee, and honour from thy presence; thou reignest over all, O Ruler of all rule; in thine hand is power and might, and in thine hand it is to make great, and to give strength unto all.—1 *Chron.* xxix. 12.

Now, therefore, our God, we thank thee, and praise thy glorious name.—*Verse* 13.

THURSDAY.

Satisfy us early with thy mercy, O Lord.—*Psalm* xc. 14.

Blessed art thou, O Lord, who, as on this day, didst bring forth out of the waters the moving creature that hath life;—*Gen.* i. 20.

The whale, and the winged fowl;—*Verse* 21.

And didst bless them, that they should be fruitful and multiply.—*Verse* 22.

The Graduals, or Steps of Ascent.

Be thou exalted, O God, above the heavens, and thy glory above all the earth.—*Psalm* cviii. 5.

As thou wast lifted up, so draw us unto thee, O Lord;—*John* xii. 32.

That we may set our affection on things above, not on things on the earth.—*Col.* iii. 2.

By the mighty mystery of thy Holy Body and thy Precious Blood, instituted on the evening of this day, have mercy on us, O Lord.—1 *Cor.* xi. 23, 24, 25.

AN ACT OF CONFESSION.

O thou, who hast said; As I live, saith the Lord God, I have no pleasure in the death of the wicked, but that the wicked turn from his way and live: turn ye, turn ye from your evil ways; for why will ye die, O house of Israel?—*Ezek.* xxxiii. 11.

Turn thou us unto thee, O Lord, and we shall be turned:—*Lament.* v. 21.

Turn us from all our transgressions, and let them not be our ruin.—*Ezek.* xviii. 30.

I have sinned, and have committed iniquity, and have done wickedly, and have rebelled, even by departing from thy precepts, and from thy judgments.—*Dan.* ix. 5.

O Lord, righteousness belongeth unto thee, but unto me confusion of face, as at this day, for the contempt wherewith thou hast despised us;—*Verse* 7.

O Lord, to us belongeth confusion of face, and to our princes, who have sinned against thee.—*Verse* 8.

O Lord, thy righteousness is in all thy works: *Verse* 14.

According to all thy righteousness, I beseech thee, let thine anger and thy fury be turned away;—*Verse* 16.

And cause thy face to shine upon thy servant.—*Verse* 17.

O my God, incline thine ear, and hear; open thine eyes, and behold my desolation.—*Verse* 18.

O Lord, hear; O Lord, forgive; O Lord, hearken; hearken, O Lord, and do; do, and defer not; for thine own sake, O Lord, O Lord my God; for thy servant is called by thy name.—*Verse* 19.

In many things we offend all.—*James* iii. 2.

Lord, let thy mercy rejoice against thy judgment of our sins.—*James* ii. 13.

If I say that I have no sin, I deceive myself, and the truth is not in me:—1 *John* i. 8.

But I confess my sins that they are many and grievous, and thou art faithful and just, O Lord, to forgive me my sins, when I confess them.—*Verse* 9.

Unto which end, moreover, I have with thee an advocate before thee, even thine only-begotten Son, the Righteous;

May he be the propitiation for my sins, who is also for the sins of the whole world.—1 *John* ii. 1, 2.

Will the Lord cast off for ever? and will he be favourable no more?—*Psalm* lxxvii. 7.

Is his mercy clean gone for ever? doth his promise fail for evermore?—*Verse* 8.

Hath God forgotten to be gracious? or will he in anger shut up his tender mercies?—*Verse* 9.

And I said, now I have begun; this change is from the right hand of the Most High.—*Ver.* 10.

A PRAYER FOR GRACE.

GRANT me, O Lord, that I may lay aside every weight, and the sin that doth so easily beset me:—*Heb.* xii. 1.

That I may lay apart all filthiness, and superfluity of naughtiness;—*James* i. 21.

The lust of the flesh, and the lust of the eyes, and the pride of life;—1 *John* ii. 16.

Every motion, whether of the flesh or of the spirit, which is repugnant to thy holy will.

The Eight Beatitudes.

LET me be poor in spirit, that mine may be the kingdom of heaven;—*Matt.* v. 3.

Let me
- mourn,
- be meek,
- hunger and thirst after righteousness,

that I may
- be comforted.
- inherit the earth.
- *Verses* 4, 5, 6.

Let me be
- merciful,
- pure in heart,
- a peacemaker,

that I may
- obtain mercy.
- see God.
- be called a child of God.
- *Verses* 7, 8, 9.

Let me be ready to suffer persecutions for righteousness' sake, that my reward may be in heaven.—*Verses* 10; 12.

AN ACT OF FAITH.

I COME unto God, believing that he is, and that he is a rewarder of them that diligently seek him.—*Heb.* xi. 6.

I know that my Redeemer liveth; *Job* xix. 25.

That he is the Christ, the Son of the living God;—*Matt.* xvi. 16.

That he is indeed the Christ, the Saviour of the world;—*John* iv. 42.

That he came into the world to save sinners, of whom I am chief.—1 *Tim.* i. 15.

I believe that through the grace of the Lord Jesus Christ I shall be saved, even as my fathers also.—*Acts* xv. 11.

I know that my skin, which suffereth corruption, shall rise again upon the earth.—*Job* xix. 26.

I believe that I shall see the goodness of the Lord in the land of the living.—*Psalm* xxvii. 13.

My heart shall rejoice in the Lord, because we have trusted in his holy name.—*Psalm* xxxiii. 21.

By thy name of
 {
  Father;
  Saviour, Mediator;
  Intercessor, Redeemer;
  Two-fold Comforter;
 }

Under thy types of
 {
  The Lamb;
  The Dove;
 }

Let thy mercy, O Lord, be upon us, according as we hope in thee.—*Psalm* xxxiii. 22.

AN ACT OF INTERCESSION.

From the Liturgies of St. Chrysostom and St. James.

LET us pray, in the peace of God, for peace from above, and for the salvation of our souls:

For the peace of the whole world; for the

stability of the holy churches of God, and the union of them all:

For this holy house, and those who enter it in faith and reverence:

For our holy fathers, the bishops; for the venerable presbytery, for the deacons ministering in Christ, and for the whole clergy and laity:

For this sacred residence; for all the city and country, and for the faithful who dwell therein:

For temperature of the heavens, for plenteousness in the fruits of the earth, and for seasons of peace:

For all who travel by land or by water; for the sick, the troubled, and the captive; for their health and safety:

Help us and save us, pity and protect us by thy grace, O God.

Neither do we forget to bless and praise thy name, for that holy, immaculate, and blessed Virgin Mary, the mother of JESUS CHRIST; and for all thy Saints;

After whose example let us commend ourselves, and one another, and our whole life, unto Christ our God;

For to thee, O Lord, belong glory, and honour, and worship.—*Rev.* iv. 11.

THE grace of our Lord Jesus Christ, the love of God, and the fellowship of the Holy Ghost, be with me, and with us all. Amen.—2 *Cor.* xiii. 14.

AND now I commend myself, my friends, and all that is mine, unto him that is able to keep me from falling, and to present me faultless before the presence of his glory;

To the only wise God, our Saviour; to whom be glory and majesty, dominion and power, both now and for ever. Amen.—*Jude*, 24, 25.

AN ACT OF PRAISE.

O LORD, my Lord, I bless thee:
  For my being,
    My life,
    My endowment with reason;
  For my nourishment,
    My preservation,
    My guidance;
  For my education,
    My civil government,
    My religion;
  For the gifts of grace,
    Of nature,
    Of the world;
  For my redemption,
    My regeneration,
    My instruction in the truth;
  For the voice of thy calling,
    Repeated often,
    Again and again;
  For thy patience,
    Thy long-suffering,

Thy very long forbearance,
Many a time and oft,
And many a year, till now;
For all the benefits I have received,
For all my undertakings which have prospered;
For all the little good I may have done;
For the enjoyment of present good,
For thy promise and my hope
Of enjoying good to come:
For my kind and honest parents,
My gentle teachers,
My benefactors, never to be forgotten;
My brethren, of one mind with me,
My congregation, who listen to me;
My relations, who are my friends,
My faithful domestics.
For all, who

By their { Writings, Sermons, Discourses, Prayers, Examples, Reproofs, Persecutions } have done me good.

For all these, and for all others,
Known or unknown,
Open or concealed,
Remembered or forgotten,
Asked or unasked,
I praise thee and will praise,

I bless thee and will bless,
I thank thee, and will give thee thanks.

Who am I, O Lord God, and what is my father's house, (2 *Sam.* vii. 18.) that thou shouldest look upon such a dead dog as I am?—2 *Sam.* ix. 8.

What reward shall I give unto the Lord, for all the benefits that he hath done unto me?—*Psalm* cxvi. 12.

What thanks can I render unto God for all things wherein he hath spared me until now?

Holy, Holy, Holy, Lord God Almighty, thou art worthy, O Lord, to receive glory, and honour, and power; for thou hast created all things, and for thy pleasure they are and were created.—*Rev.* iv. 8; 11.

FRIDAY.

In the morning shall my prayer prevent thee.—*Psalm* lxxxviii. 13.

Blessed art thou, O Lord, who, as on this day, didst bring forth from out the earth beasts, and cattle, and every creeping thing, (*Gen.* i. 24.) for food, for raiment, and for labour;

And didst make man after thine own image, that he might subdue the earth, and didst bless him.—*Gen.* i. 26. 28.

For his creation did the blessed Trinity consult together; and by thine Almighty hand was the work performed.—*Gen.* i. 26.

The breath of life was breathed into his nostrils, (*Gen.* ii. 7.) and in the image of God was he created.—*Gen.* i. 27.

Thou madest him to have dominion over thy works, (*Psalm* viii. 6.) thou gavest thy angels charge over him, (*Psalm* xci. 11.) and didst put him in the garden of Eden.—*Gen.* ii. 8.

Special Heads of Praise and Meditation.

   I. The members of the body.
       The heart, the reins,
       The eyes, the ears, the tongue,
       The hands, the feet.
   II. The faculties of the soul.
       Life, sense,

Reason, intellect, free-will,
　　　Memory, conscience.
III. The exercise of these faculties.
　　　The knowledge of God;
　　　The writings of the law;
　　　The oracles of the prophets;
　　　The melody of psalms;
　　　The instruction of proverbs;
　　　The experience of histories;
　　　The service of sacrifices.

　　BLESSED art thou, O Lord,
For thy exceeding great and precious promises,
　　　Given, as on this day,—2 *Pet.* i. 4.
　　Concerning the seed of life;—*Gen.* iii. 15.
And for the fulfilling thereof in the fulness of time,
　　Likewise upon this same day.—*Gal.* iv. 4.
　　　Blessed art thou, O Lord,
For thy holy passions of this day.
　　O, by those thy saving passions,
　　　Endured upon this day,
　　　Save us, good Lord.

AN ACT OF CONTRITION.

I HAVE rebelled against thee, O Lord;—*Hosea* xiii 16.

But I return unto thee, for I have fallen by mine iniquity;—*Hos.* xiv. 1.

But I take with me words, and turn to thee, O Lord, and say; take away all iniquity, and receive my prayer; so will I render the calves of my lips. —*Verse* 2.

Spare, O Lord, spare, and give not thine heritage to the reproach of thine enemies.—*Joel* ii. 17.

O Lord, Lord, forgive; cease; I beseech thee; by whom shall Jacob arise? for he is small.—*Amos* vii. 5.

Repent, O Lord, for this, and let it not be.—*Verse* 6.

I have observed lying vanities, and forsaken mine own mercy;—*Jonah* ii. 8.

And I am cast out of the sight of thine eyes;—*Verse* 4.

But when my soul fainted within me, I remembered the Lord.—*Verse* 7.

I will look again toward thy holy temple; let my life be brought up from corruption.—*Ver.* 4; 6.

Who is a God like unto thee, that pardonest iniquity, and passest by the transgressions of thy heritage?

Thou wilt not preserve thine anger for a continual testimony, because thou delightest in mercy. —*Micah* vii. 18.

Turn again, and have compassion on us, O Lord; subdue our iniquities, and cast all our sins into the depths of the sea;—*Verse* 19.

According to thy truth, and according to thy mercy.—*Verse* 20.

O Lord, I have heard thy speech, and was afraid; in wrath remember mercy.—*Hab.* iii. 2.

Behold me, O Lord, clothed with filthy garments, and Satan standing at my right hand.—*Zech.* iii. 3. 1.

But in the blood of thy covenant, O Lord (*Zech.* ix. 11.) in the fountain opened for the washing away of all uncleanness, (*Zech.* xiii. 1.) wash me thoroughly from mine iniquities, and cleanse me from my sin.—*Psalm* li. 2.

Save me as a brand plucked out of the fire.—*Zech.* iii. 2.

Father, forgive me; for I knew not, in truth I knew not, what I did in sinning against thee.—*Luke* xxiii. 34.

Lord, remember me in thy kingdom.—*Verse* 42.

Lord, lay not to mine enemies the charge of their sins; Lord, lay not to me the charge of mine.—*Acts* vii. 60.

But by thy drops of blood and sweat,
> Thine agony of soul;—*Luke* xxii. 44.
> Thy head crowned with thorns, and smitten with the reed;—*Matt.* xxvii. 29, 30.
> Thine eyes suffused with tears;—*Heb.* v. 7.
> Thine ears pierced with revilings;—*Matt.* xxvii. 39.
> Thy mouth moistened with vinegar and gall;—*Verse* 34.
> Thy face shamefully defiled with spitting;—*Verse* 30.
> Thy neck laden with the burthen of the cross;—*John* xix. 17.

Thy back furrowed with the scourge, with stripes and wounds;—*Psalm* cxxix. 3.

Thy hands and thy feet pierced;—*Psalm* xxii. 16.

Thy bitter crying, ELI! ELI!—*Matt.* xxvii. 46.

Thy heart pierced with the spear, the blood and water rushing out;—*John* xix. 34.

Thy body broken, and thy blood shed;

Forgive, O Lord, the iniquity of thy servant; cover all his sins:—*Psalm* lxxxv. 2.

Take away all thy wrath, turn thyself from the fierceness of thine anger.—*Verse* 3.

Turn me, O God of my salvation, and cause thine anger toward us to cease.—*Verse* 4.

Wilt thou be angry with us for ever? or wilt thou stretch out thy wrath from one generation to another?—*Verse* 5.

O God, thou shalt turn again, and quicken us; and thy people shall rejoice in thee.—*Verse* 6.

Shew us thy mercy, O Lord, and grant us thy salvation.—*Verse* 7.

A PRAYER FOR GRACE.

LET me walk in the Spirit, O God, that I may not fulfil the lust of the flesh.—*Gal.* v. 16.

Now the works of the flesh are these:
Adultery, fornication, uncleanness, lasciviousness;
Idolatry, witchcraft;
Hatred, variance, emulations;

Wrath, strife;
Seditions, heresies;
Envyings, murders, drunkenness, revellings,
And such like.—*Verses* 19, 20, 21.
But the fruits of the Spirit are
Love, joy, peace;
Long-suffering, gentleness, goodness;
Faith, meekness, temperance.—*Verses* 22, 23.
Let thy Spirit, O Lord, rest upon me;
The Spirit of wisdom and understanding,
The Spirit of counsel and might,
The Spirit of knowledge and holiness,
And of the fear of the Lord.—*Isai.* xi. 2.

Give me, O Lord, the manifestations of thy Spirit, that I may profit withal.—1 *Cor.* xii. 7.
The gifts of the Spirit are
The word of wisdom,
The word of knowledge;
Faith, with the gift of healing,
Faith, with the working of miracles;
Prophecy, and the discerning of spirits;
Divers kinds of tongues,
The interpretation of tongues.—*Verses* 4; 8, 9, 10.

AN ACT OF FAITH.

LORD, I believe,
That thou didst create me:
Forsake not the work of thine own hands.
—*Psalm* cxxxviii. 8.

That thou madest me after thine own image and
   likeness;—*Gen.* i. 26.
Suffer not thine own likeness to be blotted out.
That thou didst redeem me by thy blood:—*Rev.*
   v. 9.
Suffer not the purchase of thy redemption to
   perish.
That thou hast called me CHRISTIAN after thine
   own name:—*Acts* xi. 26.
Despise not one who bears thy name.
That thou hast sanctified me in the washing of
   regeneration:—*Titus* iii. 5.
Destroy not that which thou hast made holy.
That thou didst graft me into the good olive-tree,
   (*Rom.* xi. 24.) a member of a mystical body:
   —*Eph.* v. 30.
Cut not off a branch of thine own body mystical.

REMEMBER thy word unto thy servant, upon
which thou hast caused me to hope.—*Psalm* cxix.
49.

My soul fainteth for thy salvation, but I hope in
thy word.—*Verse* 81.

AN ACT OF INTERCESSION.

LET us pray
For the successful warfare and increase of every
   Christian army, against the enemies of our most
   holy faith.
For our holy Fathers, and all brethren in Christ.

For those who hate, and those who love us.
For those who pity us, and minister unto our wants.
For those whom we have promised to remember in our prayers.
For the liberation of all who are in bonds.
For our absent fathers and families.
For those who traverse the wide ocean.
For those who are bending under infirmity.

LET us commemorate
Religious kings, and prelates in the church;
The founders of this holy building;
Our parents, and all our forefathers and brethren, who are gone before us.

LET thy mighty hand, O Lord, be ever with me for protection;
Thy mercy in Christ for my salvation;
Thine unerring word for my instruction;
The grace of thy quickening Spirit for my comfort, even unto the end, and in the end.

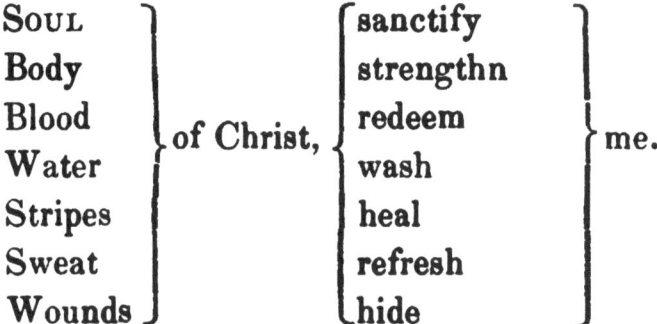

The peace of God which passeth all understanding, keep my heart and mind in the knowledge and love of God.— *Philip.* iv. 7.

AN ACT OF PRAISE.

From the Liturgy of St. James.

MOST gracious God, who didst not despise nor abandon man after he had transgressed thy law, and fallen;

But like an indulgent father didst visit him in many ways;

Giving him thy great and precious promise of the seed of life;—*Gen.* iii. 15.

Opening to him the door of faith and repentance unto life;—*Acts* xiv. 27.

And in the fulness of time sending the same thy Christ, (*Ibid.*) to take on him the seed of Abraham;—*Heb.* ii. 16.

And by the oblation of his life to fulfil the obedience of the law;

And by the sacrifice of his death to take away the curse thereof;

By his death to redeem the world, and by his resurrection to restore the same unto life:

Thou who doest all things to bring back mankind to thee, that he may be made partaker of thy divine nature, and share thy everlasting glory;

Who hast borne testimony to the truth of thy gospel by numerous and manifold signs;

By the ever-memorable conduct of thy saints; by their miraculous endurance of tortures; by the astonishing conversion of the whole world unto the obedience of the faith, without the aid of arms, of eloquence, of power;

Blessed, and praised, and celebrated, and magnified, and exalted, and glorified, and hallowed be thy name, thy memory and mention, and every memorial of thy love, both now and for ever.

THOU art worthy to take the book, and to open the seals thereof; for thou wast slain and hast redeemed us to God by thy blood, out of every kindred and tongue, and people, and nation;— *Rev.* v. 9.

Worthy is the Lamb, that was slain, to receive power, and riches, and wisdom, and strength, and honour, and glory, and blessing.—*Verse* 12.

Blessing, and honour, and glory, and power, be unto him that sitteth upon the throne, and unto the Lamb, for ever and ever. Amen.—*Verses* 13, 14.

Salvation to our God, which sitteth upon the throne, and unto the Lamb. Amen.—*Rev.* vii. 10.

Blessing, and glory, and wisdom, and thanksgiving, and honour, and power, and might, be unto our God, for ever and ever. Amen.—*Verse* 12.

SATURDAY.

O Lord, be gracious unto us, for we have waited for thee; be thou our arm every morning, our salvation also in the time of trouble.—*Isaiah* xxxiii. 2.

Blessed art thou, O Lord, who, on the seventh day, didst rest from all thy work, and didst bless and sanctify it.—*Gen.* ii. 2, 3.

Heads of Meditation and Devotion.

The institution and rites of the Sabbath.
Our intervals of rest on its return.
The death and resurrection of Christ.
The consequent absolution from sin.
The example of those, who are gone before us to their rest.

AN ACT OF CONFESSION.

O my God, I am ashamed and blush to lift up my face to thee; for mine iniquities are increased over my head, and my trespass is grown up unto the heavens.—*Ezra* ix. 6.

Since the days of my youth I have been in a great trespass unto this day, (*Verse* 7) neither can I stand before thee because of this.—*Verse* 15.

From the Prayer of Manasses.

I have sinned above the number of the sands of the sea; my transgressions are multiplied; and I am not worthy to behold and see the height of heaven for the multitude of mine iniquities:

Neither can I take my breath; for 1 have provoked thy wrath, and done evil before thee; I did not thy will, neither kept I thy commandments.

Now, therefore, I bow the knee of my heart, beseeching grace of thee.

I have sinned, O Lord, I have sinned, and I acknowledge mine iniquities; wherefore, I humbly beseech thee, forgive me, O Lord, forgive me, and destroy me not with mine iniquities.

*Be not angry with me for ever, by reserving evil for me; neither condemn me into the lower parts of the earth.

For thou art the God, even the God of them that repent, and in me thou wilt shew all thy goodness; for thou wilt save me that am unworthy, according to thy great mercy.

Therefore I will praise thee for ever, all the days of my life.

A PRAYER FOR GRACE.

LORD, if thou wilt, thou canst make me clean.—*Matt.* viii. 2.

LORD, speak the word only, and I shall be healed.—*Verse* 8.

Lord, save me.—*Matt.* xiv. 30.

Carest thou not that we perish?—*Mark* iv. 38.

Say unto me, Be of good cheer; thy sins be forgiven thee.—*Matt.* ix. 2.

Jesus, Master, have mercy on me.—*Luke* xvii. 13.

Jesus, thou Son of David, have mercy on me.—*Mark* x. 47.

Jesus, thou Son of David, thou Son of David.—*Verse* 48.

Lord, say unto me, Ephphatha.—*Mark* vii. 34.

Lord, I have no man to help me.—*John* v. 7.

Lord, say unto me, Thou art loosed from thine infirmity.—*Luke* xiii. 12.

Say unto my soul, I am thy salvation.—*Psalm* xxxv. 3.

Say unto me, My grace is sufficient for thee.—2 *Cor.* xii. 9.

How long, Lord, wilt thou be angry? for ever? and shall thy jealousy burn like fire?—*Psalm* lxxix. 5.

Remember not our former iniquities; let thy tender mercies speedily prevent us; for we are brought very low.—*Verse* 8.

Help us, O God of our salvation, for the glory of thy name; O Lord, deliver us, and purge away our sins, for thy name's sake.—*Verse* 9.

In all my faults,
My defects, my errors, my offences,
My falls, my stumblings, my transgressions,
My debts, my sins, my wickednesses,
My ignorances, my iniquities,
My impieties, my unrighteousnesses, my abominations;
The guilt

Forgive, pardon, remit, and overlook;
  Be merciful and spare;
Impute not, arraign not, remember not.
     The stain
    Pass by, pass over,
  Look beside, look beyond,
Conceal, wash off, blot out, and purge away.
     The disease
  Dismiss, heal, make whole,
  Remove, receive, relieve,
    Abolish, frustrate, and disperse.
Let them not be found: let them not exist.

    Give me all diligence to add

To my faith	virtue,
To my virtue	knowledge,
To my knowledge	temperance,
To my temperance	patience,
To my patience	godliness,
To my godliness	brotherly-kindness,
To my brotherly-kindness	charity.—*2 Pet.* i. 5, 6, 7.

Let me not forget that I have been purged from my old sins, but give diligence by good works to make my calling and election sure.—*Verses* 9, 10.

AN ACT OF FAITH.

I BELIEVE in thee, THE FATHER:

Behold, then, if thou be a Father, and we be children, like as a father pitieth his children, so pity thou us, O Lord.—*Psalm* ciii. 13.

I believe in thee, THE LORD:

Behold, then, if thou be Lord, and we be servants, our eyes wait upon thee, our Lord, until thou have mercy upon us.—*Psalm* cxxiii. 2.

I believe that, although we were neither children nor servants, but only dogs, we might yet be allowed to eat of the crumbs which fall from thy table.—*Matt.* xv. 27.

I believe that CHRIST is the LAMB OF GOD:

O Lamb of God, that takest away the sins of the world, take away mine also.—*John* i. 29.

I believe that Jesus Christ came into the world to save sinners:

Thou, who camest to save sinners, save me also, the first and the chief of sinners.—1 *Tim.* i. 15.

I believe that Christ came to save that which was lost:

Thou who camest to save that which was lost, suffer not that to be lost, which thou hast saved.—*Matt.* xviii. 11.

I believe that the HOLY GHOST is the Lord and Giver of Life:—*Nicene Creed.*

Thou who hast given me a living soul, (*Gen.* ii. 7.) grant that I may not receive my soul in vain.

I believe that the Spirit imparteth grace in his holy mysteries:

Grant that I receive not his grace, nor the hope of his blessed sacraments, in vain.—2 *Cor.* vi. 1.

I believe that the Spirit himself maketh intercession for us with groanings which cannot be uttered;

Of that his intercession, and of those his unutterable groanings, make me partaker, O Lord.—*Rom.* viii. 26.

OUR fathers trusted in thee; they trusted, and thou didst deliver them.—*Psalm* xxii. 4.

They cried unto thee, and were delivered; they trusted in thee, and were not confounded.—*Verse* 5.

As in the old time thou didst deliver our fathers, so likewise deliver us, O Lord, who put our trust in thee.—*Psalm* xxxiii. 11.

AN ACT OF INTERCESSION.

O HEAVENLY KING,
Strengthen our Christian rulers,
Establish the true faith,
Assuage the wrath of the heathen,
Give peace unto the world,
Graciously protect this pious institution,
And, according to thy goodness and love toward man,
Receive us in thy faith and penitence.

MAY the Power of the Father govern me.
May the Wisdom of the Son enlighten me.
May the Operation of the Holy Spirit quicken me.

O GOD, I beseech thee,
Guard my soul;
Sustain my body;

Exalt my senses;
Direct my course;
Regulate my manners;
Bless my undertakings;
Fulfil my petitions;
Inspire me with holy thoughts;
Pardon what is past;
Rectify what is present;
Order what is to come.

AN ACT OF PRAISE.

Now unto him that is able to do exceeding abundantly above all that we ask or think, according to the power that worketh in us;

Unto Him be glory in the church, by Christ Jesus, throughout all ages, world without end. Amen.—*Eph.* iii. 20, 21.

BLESSED, praised, celebrated, magnified, exalted, glorified, and hallowed be thy name, O Lord, the remembrance, and the mention, and every memorial of it:

For the most honourable senate of patriarchs
The ever-venerable band of prophets;
The most famous company of thy twelve apostles; and of the evangelists;
The noble army of martyrs and ministers;
The assembly of doctors and professors;
The beautiful devotion of virgins;
The sweet innocence of children:
For their faith and hope;

Their labours and truth;
Their bravery and zeal;
Their learning and seclusion;
Their chastity and simplicity.

GLORY to thee, O Lord, glory to thee;
Glory to thee, who hast glorified those, in whom we also glorify thee.

Great and marvellous are thy works, Lord God Almighty; just and true are thy ways, thou King of Saints.—*Rev.* xv. 3.

Who shall not fear thee, O Lord, and glorify thy name? for thou only art holy: for all nations shall come and worship before thee; for thy judgments are made manifest.—*Verse* 4.

Praise our God, all ye his servants, and ye that fear him both small and great.—*Rev.* xix. 5.

Hallelujah! for the Lord our God Omnipotent reigneth.—*Verse* 6.

Let us be glad, and rejoice, and give honour to him.—*Verse* 7.

Behold, the tabernacle of God is with men, and he will dwell with them, and they shall be his people, and God himself shall be with them.—*Rev.* xxi. 3.

And he shall wipe away all tears from their eyes; and there shall be no more death, neither sorrow, nor crying, neither shall there be any more pain; for the former things are passed away.—*Verse* 4.

A FORM OF PRAYER

For all the World, and particularly for our special Relations.

Do good, O Lord, and visit in thy mercy
  The universe, and all thy creatures;
  The earth, and all mankind.
  The states of the world.
  Christianity and the Catholic Church;
  All churches and states in particular;
  Our own church and state.
  The various ranks, ecclesiastical and civil,
      In this country;
  And, in those ranks, the persons
      Of our king and nobles,
         And of the priesthood.
The City of London, wherein I was born;
The Parish of *All-Hallows, Barking,* wherein I was baptized;
The two Academies of *Merchant Tailors* and *St. Paul's;*
The University and College, wherein I was brought up;
The Parish of *St. Giles, Cripplegate,* entrusted to my charge;
  Pembroke Hall, at Cambridge;
  The three Churches of { Southwell, St. Paul's, and Westminster;

The three Bishopricks of { Chichester, Ely, and Winchester.

My family and kindred.
Those who have shewn compassion,
Those who have ministered, to me.
  My neighbours and friends.
    Those commended to my prayers.

A RECOMMENDATION

Of Ourselves and our Concerns to God's Blessing.

O LORD, I commit unto thee
  My { soul and body, mind and thoughts;
  My { vows and prayers, senses and limbs;
  My { words and works, life and death.
My brethren and sisters, with their children.
  My { benefactors and well-wishers; kindred and neighbours; native country.
  All Christian people.
O Lord, I commit unto thee
  My { designs and attempts, resolutions and undertakings;
  My { going out and coming in, sitting down and rising up.

PRAYERS PREPARATORY TO EVERY THANKSGIVING.

Thou, O God, art worthy to be praised; and unto thee shall the vow be performed.—*Psalm* clxv. 1.

Thou art worthy, O Lord, our blessed God, to receive glory, and honour, and power.—*Rev.* iv. 11.

Thou that hearest the prayer, unto thee shall all flesh come; even mine own shall come.—*Ps.* lxv. 2.

But the words of the ungodly prevail against me; as to my transgressions, thou shalt be merciful unto them:—*Verse* 3.

That I may come and praise thee with all thy works, and bless thee with thy saints.—*Psalm* cxlv. 10.

Thou shalt open my lips, O Lord, and my mouth shall shew forth thy praise.—*Psalm* li. 15.

A FORM OF THANKSGIVING

For Temporal and Spiritual Blessings.

My soul doth magnify the Lord,—*Luke* i. 46.
  Because he hath dealt favourably
    With all his creatures,
    With all mankind.
  Because he hath shewed mercy unto me,
  With regard to my soul, my body, my means of life,
    In the gifts of grace, of nature, and of the world.

With regard to all the benefits I have received,

With regard to the many undertakings Wherein I have succeeded and do succeed.

With regard to any benefit I may perhaps have conferred on others.

I praise God

For my
- health,
- reputation,
- contentment,
- safety,
- freedom,
- peace.

Thou hast not cut off, like a weaver, my life, while it was yet beginning: neither hast thou made an end of me from day even to night.—*Isaiah* xxxviii. 12.

Thou hast given me life and breath even to this hour: from my childhood and my youth until now; even until old age and grey hairs.—*Psalm* lxxi. 15, 16.

Hold my soul in life, and suffer not my foot to be moved.—*Psalm* lxvi. 9.

For thou hast delivered me

From
- Dangers,
- Diseases,
- Poverty,
- Servitude,
- Public shame,
- Evil accidents.

Thou hast not given me up to perish in my iniquity, but ever waited for my conversion: and thou hast still left in me

Communion with my heart;

A remembrance of the four last ends,

Of death, of judgment, of heaven, of hell;

Some shame, and horror, and remorse

For my sins past:

O, that I felt it more and oftener, more and oftener,

Continually more vehement, O Lord!

And thou hast given me good hope for the remission of my sins, by repentance, and by the works of repentance, by the power of the holy keys, and of the sacraments administered in thy church.

So that, from day to day, for these thy mercies vouchsafed to me, which I forget not; and also for many more forgotten by reason of their number and my unmindfulness;

Conferred on me,

Whether knowing, willing, and asking;

Or neither asking, willing, nor knowing;

For all of them

I confess and offer thanks to thee;

I bless and praise thee daily, as is meet;

I pray unto thee with all my soul;

I pray unto thee with all my mind.

Glory be to thee, O Lord,

Glory be to thee;

Glory be to thee,
And glory to thy most holy name,
For all thy heavenly attributes :
For thy unspeakable and incomparable goodness, and thy mercy toward sinners and the unworthy; even unto me the most unworthy sinner of all.
For these, and for all thy other mercies,
Be glory, and honour, and praise,
And blessing, and thanksgiving unto thee,
With the voices, and concert of voices,
Of angels and of men,
And of all thy saints in heaven,
And of all thy creatures in heaven and earth ;
And beneath the feet of all,
From me, a worthless and miserable sinner,
The poorest of thy creatures ;
Now, on this day, at this hour,
And every day unto my latest breath,
Yea, unto the end of the world,
And for ever and ever. Amen.

A LITANY, OR DEPRECATION,

To be used upon Special Occasions of Public or Private Humiliation.

O FATHER, who dost create,
Destroy not him whom thou hast created.
O SON, who dost redeem,
Destroy not him whom thou hast redeemed.
O SPIRIT, who dost regenerate,

Destroy not him whom thou hast regenerated.

Remember not, Lord, my offences, nor the offences of my forefathers, neither take thou vengeance of our sins, whether theirs or mine. Spare us, good Lord, spare them and me; spare thy people, and in thy people, me thy servant, whom thou hast redeemed with thy precious blood, and be not angry with us for ever.—*Liturgy*.

Be merciful, be merciful, spare us, O Lord, and be not angry with us for ever.

Be merciful, be merciful, pity us, O Lord, and be not angry with us too sorely.

Deal not, O Lord, deal not with me after my sins; neither reward me according to mine iniquities;—*Psalm* ciii. 10.

But deal with me according to thy great mercy, and reward me after the multitude of thy compassions:

Even according to that great mercy, and after that multitude of compassions, whereafter thou didst deal with our fathers in the generations of old.

Rescue me, by all that is dear and acceptable unto thee, preserve me from all evil and adversity,

 At every period of necessity;

From this evil and adversity in particular,

 At this special moment.

Deliver me, O Lord, and destroy me not.

 On the bed of sickness,

 In the hour of death,

At the day of judgment,—*Liturgy*.
That terrible and dreadful day,
    Rescue me, O Lord, and save me:
That I behold not the stern aspect of my Judge;—
    Rev. vi. 16.
That I be not placed upon the left hand;
That I hear not that horrible sentence,
    Depart from me:—*Matt.* xxv. 33; 41.
That I be not bound in chains of darkness;—
        2 *Pet.* ii. 4. *Jude* 6.
        cast into outer darkness;—*Matt.* xxv. 30.
        tormented in the lake of fire and brimstone, where the smoke of torments ascendeth up for ever and ever.—*Rev.* xiv. 10, 11.
    Be merciful, be merciful;
        Spare us,
Have compassion upon us, O Lord;
    And destroy us not for ever,
        Not for ever, O Lord.
And that this may not happen to me,
    Take away from me, O Lord,
(1. *The Six Fore-runners of Sin against the Holy Ghost,*)

Hardness of heart;—*Mark* xvi. 14.
Want of feeling for sins committed;—*Eph.* iv. 19.
Blindness of heart;—*Verse* 18.
A disregard for thy threatenings;—*Prov.* i. 24.
A conscience seared, as with a hot iron;—1 *Tim.* iv. 2.

A reprobate mind.—*Rom.* i. 28.
2. Sin against the Holy Ghost;—*Matt.* xii. 32.
    Sin unto death.—1 *John* v. 16.
      (3. *The Four Crying Sins.*)
Wilful murder;—*Gen.* iv. 10.
Unnatural lusts;—*Gen.* xix. 5.
Oppression of the fatherless and widow;—*Exod.* xxii. 22.
Detention of the wages of the labourer.—*James* v. 4.

From all the evils and perils of this world;
  From pestilence, famine, and war;
  From earthquakes, floods, and fires;
  From immoderate rain or drought;
  From blight and mildew;
  From thunder, lightning, and tempest;
  From spreading, painful, and malignant disorders,
  And from sudden death,
      Good Lord, deliver us.
From atrocious evils in the church;
  From private interpretations of Scripture;—2 *Pet.* i. 20.
  From innovation in holy things;—*Acts* xvii. 21.
  From the teaching of strange doctrines;—1 *Tim.* i. 3.
  From doting about questions, and strifes of words;—1 *Tim.* vi. 4.
  From heresies, schisms, and offences, public and private;
      Good Lord, deliver us.

From the deifying of kings;—*Acts* xii. 22.
From adulation of the people;—*Mark* xv. 15. *Acts* xii. 3. *and* xxiv. 27.
From the unconcernedness of Saul;—1 *Sam.* xv. 9.
From the scorn of Michal;—2 *Sam.* vi. 16.
And from the fleshhook of Hophni;—1 *Sam.* ii. 13.

  Good Lord, deliver us.

From the massacre of Athaliah;—2 *Kings* xi. 1.
From the priesthood of Micah;—*Judges* xvii. 10.
From the covenants of Simon and of Judas;— *Acts* viii. 18. *and Matt.* xxvi. 15.

  Good Lord, deliver us.

From the doctrine of the unlearned and unstable; —2 *Pet.* iii. 16.
From the pride of novices;—1 *Tim.* iii. 6.
From the people that strive with the priest;— *Hosea* iv. 4.

  Good Lord, deliver us.

From atrocious evils in the state;
From anarchy, polycracy, and tyranny;
From Ashur, Jeroboam, Rehoboam, Gallio, and Haman;—*Gen.* x. 11, 12. 1 *Kings* xv. 30. 1 *Kings* xii. 15. *Acts* xviii. 17. *Esther* iii. 6.

  Good Lord, deliver us.

From the counsel of Achitophel;—2 *Sam.* xvi. 21.
From the foolish counsellors of Zoan;—*Isaiah* xix. 11.
From the statutes of Omri;—*Micah* vi. 16.

From the rulers of Jezreel ;—2 *Kings* x. 1.
From the floods of Belial ;—*Ps.* xviii. 4.
From the plague of Peor ;—*Numb.* xxv. 5.
From the valley of Achor ;—*Josh.* vii. 26.
   Good Lord, deliver us.
From contamination of blood or seed ;
From hostile invasion, and civil war ;
From the removal of good men from authority,
And the exaltation of the wicked and deceitful
 into office,
   Good Lord, deliver us.
From life, that hath no life in it,
In tribulation and infirmity ;
In ill report and poverty ;
In danger, slavery, and disquietude ;
   Good Lord, deliver us.
 From death,
In sin or shame,
In torture of body, or distraction of mind,
In ignominy or violence,
Or in recompense of treason ;
  From sudden death,
  And from eternal death,
   Good Lord, deliver us.

HOSANNAH IN THE HIGHEST:

A Supplication for Spiritual Blessings.

REMEMBER me, O Lord, with the favour that thou
  bearest unto thy people;
Visit me with thy salvation;
  That I may see the good of thy chosen;
  That I may rejoice in the gladness of thy nation;
  That I may glory with thine inheritance.—
    Psalm cvi. 4, 5.

BUT there is a glory that shall be revealed;—
1 *Pet.* v. 1.

For there be some who, when the Judge cometh, shall see his face with joy;—*Job* xxxiii. 26.

Who shall be set on his right hand, and hear that most sweet voice,
  Come, ye blessed!—*Matt.* xxv. 33, 34.

Who shall be caught up to meet the Lord in the clouds;—1 *Thess.* iv. 17.

Who shall enter into his joy;—*Matt.* xxv. 21.

Who shall enjoy the vision of him; who shall ever be with him.—1 *Thess.* iv. 17.

These only, only these, are blessed among the sons of men:

O! give to me, the meanest of them all, the meanest place beneath their feet, beneath the feet of thine elect, of the meanest of them.

AND to this end, let me find grace in thy sight, that I may have grace, whereby I may serve thee acceptably, with reverence and godly fear.—*Heb.* xii. 28.

But let me also find this other grace, that I receive not that grace in vain, (2 *Cor.* vi. 1.) nor fall short of it :—*Heb.* xii. 15.
Much less that I neglect it,—1 *Tim.* iv. 14.
 So as utterly to fall from it ;—*Gal.* v. 4.
But that I stir it up,—2 *Tim.* i. 6.
 So as to grow in it ;—2 *Pet.* iii. 18.
Nay, that I continue therein—*Acts* xiii. 43.
 To the very end of my life.
And O, perfect that which is lacking—1 *Thess.* iii. 10.
 Of thy graces :
1. Of Faith; increase my slender faith :—*Luke* xvii. 5.
2. Of Hope; confirm my trembling hope :—*Heb.* iii. 6.
3. Of Charity; kindle the smoking flax thereof.— *Matt.* xii. 20.

Shed abroad in my heart the love of thee,—*Rom.* v. 5.
 That, like unto thee, I may love
  My friend in thee,
  My foe for thy sake.
O thou who givest grace unto the humble,—*James* iv. 6.
 Give me also grace to be humble.
O thou who never failest them that fear thee, let my heart rejoice to fear thee,—*Psalm* lxxxvi. 11.
 My fear and my hope ;—*Job* iv. 6

One thing only let me fear, that I fear any thing more than thee.

As I would that men should do unto me, may I also do unto them :—*Luke* vi. 31.

Nor let me think of myself more highly than I ought to think, but think soberly.—*Rom.* xii. 3.

Give light to them that sit in darkness and in the shadow of death: guide our feet into the way of peace :—*Luke* i. 79.

That we may be like-minded one toward another; —*Rom.* xv. 5.

That we may rightly divide the word of truth; —2 *Tim.* ii. 15.

That we may walk uprightly ;—*Gal.* ii. 14.

That we may edify one another ;—1 *Thess.* v. 11.

That we may with one mind and one mouth glorify God.—*Rom.* xv. 6.

Nevertheless, if in any thing we be otherwise minded,

That, whereto we have already attained, we may walk by the same rule ;—*Phil.* iii. 15, 16.

That we may do all things decently and in order, —1 *Cor.* xiv. 40.

And with steadfastness of faith.—*Coloss.* ii. 5.

HOSANNAH UPON EARTH:

A Supplication for Temporal Blessings.

REMEMBER, O Lord, to crown the year with thy goodness.—*Psalm* lxv. 11.

For the eyes of all wait upon thee, and thou givest them their meat in due season.—*Ps.* cxlv. 15.

Thou openest thine hand, and fillest all things living with plenteousness.—*Verse* 16.

And vouchsafe unto us, O Lord,
The precious things of heaven, the dew from above;
The blessing of the fountains of the deep from beneath;
The courses of the sun,
The circuits of the moon;
The heights of the mountains of the East,
Of the ancient hills;
The blessings of the earth, and the fulness thereof.—*Deut.* xxxiii. 13, 14, 15, 16.

Vouchsafe unto us
Seasons of fertility, temperature of atmosphere,
Abundant supplies of corn and fruits,
Health of body, and days of peace;
Upright rulers, and a prosperous government;
Equal laws, and righteous judgments;
Honesty in our judges,
Obedience in the people,
Fortitude in the magistracy, and
Plenteousness in the provisions of life:
Happy births, and numerous offspring,
Offspring, lovely in form and nature,
Nursed in strength, and trained in godliness:
That our sons may be as plants, grown up in their youth; that our daughters may be polished after the similitude of a palace;
That our garners may be full, affording all manner of store; that our sheep may bring forth

thousands, and our oxen may be strong to labour;

That there be no breaking in, nor going out, nor complaining in our streets.—*Ps.* cxliv. 12, 13, 14.

One thing have I desired of the Lord, that will I seek after; that I may dwell in the house of the Lord all the days of my life, to behold the beauty of the Lord, and to visit his holy temple.—*Psalm* xxvii. 4.

Two things have I required of thee, O Lord; deny me them not before I die:

Remove far from me vanity and lies; give me neither poverty nor riches; feed me but with food convenient for me:

Lest perhaps I be filled, and puffed up, and say, Who is the Lord? or lest I be driven by poverty to steal, and take the name of my God in vain.—*Prov.* xxx. 7, 8, 9.

Let me learn to abound, and let me learn to be abased, and, in whatsoever state I am, therewith to be content.—*Phil.* iv. 11, 12.

But beyond what I possess, let me neither desire nor at any time expect any thing earthly, transitory, or corruptible.

Grant me a comfortable life, in godliness, sobriety, and chastity, in all goodness, in cheerfulness of mind, in health of body, in fair reputation, with contentment, with safety and freedom, in an age of peace.

Grant me a happy death, and a life of immortality.

EVENING PRAYERS AND MEDITATIONS.

HAVING passed over this day, I give thanks unto thee, O Lord.

The evening draweth nigh; make thou it comfortable.

As the day hath its evening, so also hath the life of man: the evening of life is old age.

Old age hath taken hold of me; make this also comfortable.

Cast me not off in the time of old age; forsake me not when my strength faileth.—*Psalm* lxxi. 9.

Even to mine old age be thou he, and even to hoar hairs carry me; do thou make, and do thou bear; thou shalt carry and deliver me, O Lord.—*Isaiah* xlvi. 4.

Abide with me, for it is toward evening, and the day of this toilsome life is now far spent.—*Jer.* vi. 4.

Let thy strength be made perfect in my weakness.—2 *Cor.* xii. 9.

THE day is vanished and gone; my life also is vanished, a life wherein we scarcely live.

The night cometh on, death also cometh on; a death wherein we shall not die.

As is the end of the day, even so is the end of life, even near at hand.

We, therefore, remembering this, beseech thee, O Lord, to grant that our ends may be truly Christian, acceptable to thee, void of sin and shame, and, so far as thou shalt think proper, void of pain.

Guide us in peace, O Lord our Lord, gathering us together under the feet of thine elect, when thou wilt, and as thou wilt, only without shame and sin.

LET me remember the days of darkness, for they are many:—*Eccles.* xi. 8.

That I be not cast into outer darkness.—*Matt.* xxii. 13.

Let me remember and prevent the night, by working some good work.—*John* ix. 4.

The judgment is at hand: grant, O Lord, that we may give a good and acceptable account at the dread and terrible tribunal of JESUS CHRIST.

I LIFT up my hands by night in the sanctuary, and bless the Lord.—*Psalm* cxxxiv. 2, 3.

The Lord hath commanded his loving-kindness in the day-time, and in the night his song shall be with me, and my prayer unto the God of my life. —*Psalm* xlii. 8.

Thus will I bless thee while I live, and I will lift up my hands in thy name.—*Psalm* lxiii. 4.

Let my prayer be set forth before thee as incense; the lifting up of my hands as the evening sacrifice.—*Psalm* cxli. 2.

Blessed art thou, O Lord our God, the God of our fathers;

Who didst create the successions of day and night;—*Gen.* i. 14.

Who givest songs in the night;—*Job* xxxv. 10.

Who hast delivered us from the evil of this day;—*Matt.* vi. 13.

Who hast not cut off, like a weaver, my life, neither from morning even to night hast thou made an end of me.—*Isaiah* xxxviii. 12.

A CONFESSION OF SIN.

Lord, as we add days unto days, so we add sins unto sins.—*Ecclus.* v. 5.

A just man falleth seven times a day;—*Prov.* xxiv. 16.

But I, a wretched sinner, fall seventy times seven:—*Matt.* xviii. 22.

A wonderful and horrible thing, O Lord!—*Jer.* v. 30.

But I return with groaning from my wicked ways, (*Ezek.* xx. 44.) and return unto my heart, (*Jer.* xxiv. 7.) and return unto thee with my whole heart, (*Deut.* xxx. 2.) O God of the penitent, and Saviour of sinners!—1 *Tim.* i. 15.

And evening after evening I will return: from the inmost recesses of my heart, and out of the depths, my soul crieth unto thee.—*Psalm* cxxx. 1.

Lord, I have sinned against thee, grievously I have sinned against thee; have mercy, alas! alas! have mercy on my wretchedness.

I repent; woe is me! I repent; spare me, O Lord! I repent; woe is me! I repent: help thou my lack of repentance.—*Mark* ix. 24.

Have pity, O Lord, and spare me: have pity, and be merciful unto me.

I said; Lord be merciful unto me; heal my soul, for I have sinned against thee.—*Ps.* xli. 4.

Have mercy upon me, O God, after thy great goodness, and according to the multitude of thy mercies do away mine offences.—*Psalm* li. 1.

> Forgive my guilt,
> Heal my sores,
> Blot out my spots,
> Rescue me from shame,
> Deliver me from servitude,
> And make me not an example to my fellows.

BRING me out of my distresses, O Lord;—*Ps.* xxv. 17.

Cleanse thou me from secret faults;—*Psalm* xix. 12.

And keep back thy servant from presumptuous sins.—*Verse* 13.

Impute not unto me the wanderings of concupiscence, (*Wisd.* iv. 12.) nor every idle word.—*Matt.* xii. 36.

Turn aside the black and filthy tide of unclean and unlawful thoughts.

O Lord, my destruction is of myself.—*Hosea* xiii. 9.

Graciously pardon whatever I have done amiss.—*Neh.* ix. 17.

Deal not with us after our sins, neither reward us according to our iniquities.—*Psalm* ciii. 10.

Graciously look upon our infirmities, and, for the glory of thy most holy name, turn from us all those evils, which are most righteously due to our sins, and for them to us.—*Liturgy.*

AT THE APPROACH OF NIGHT.

Give rest also, O Lord, to me that droop; renew my strength, for I am weary.

Lighten mine eyes, lest I sleep the sleep of death.—*Psalm* xiii. 3.

Deliver me from the terror by night, from the pestilence that walketh in darkness.—*Ps.* xci. 5, 6.

Grant me wholesome sleep, and to pass this night without fear.

O thou Keeper of Israel, who neither slumberest nor sleepest;—*Psalm* cxxi. 4.

Preserve me this night from all evil, preserve my soul, O Lord.—*Verse* 7.

Visit me with the salvation of thy saints; (*Ps.* cvi. 4.) and open my understanding in the visions of the night.—*Job* xxxiii. 15, 16.

But if not so, (for I am unworthy, I am unworthy,) at least, good Lord, let my sleep be a cessation, as from labour, so also from sin; even so, O Lord.

Neither in my dreams let me imagine aught that may offend thee or defile myself.

Let not my loins be filled with illusions;—*Psalm* xxxviii. 7.

But let my reins instruct me in the night-season;—*Psalm* xvi. 7.

Yet without grievous fear.

Preserve me from the dismal sleep of sin, and quiet every earthly and wicked thought within me.

Give me sweet repose, free from every carnal and devilish imagination.

Thou well knowest, O Lord, how watchful are my unseen enemies; thou knowest the infirmity of my sinful flesh, for thou hast made me.—*Psalm* ciii. 14.

Let the wings of thy mercy protect me.—*Psalm* xvii. 8. *and* xci. 4.

Raise me up again in a time when thou mayest be found, at the hour of prayer;—*Psalm* xxxii. 6.

And let me awake right early (*Psalm* cviii. 2.) to praise and worship thee.

BLESS, O Lord,
Thy creatures, mankind;
Those in poverty and those in wealth,
Those in error and those in truth,
Those in sin and those in grace.
Bless the Universal Church;
The Eastern, the Western, our own;
Prelates, clergy, and laity.

Bless all the governments of the earth,
Particularly those of Christianity,
 Our neighbours' and our own.
  Bless the king,
 And all the royal family.
  Bless the nobles,
 The council, the magistrates, and officers.
  Bless the people,
 Husbandmen, merchants, artificers,
Even to poor mechanics and beggars.
Bless all those who are entitled to my prayers
 By kindred, or
 Kindness shewn to me in the ministration of worldly matters.
 By any charge, in times past or times present, committed to me.
 By moral friendship; Christian charity;
  Vicinity of habitation.
 By my own promise, or their request;
 By their own want of leisure;
 By my pity for their distresses;
 By their occupation in some arduous pursuit for the benefit of mankind;
 By some offence I have given to them;
 By the want of any other to intercede for them.

AT BED-TIME.

INTO thy hands, O Lord, I commit myself;
 My spirit, my soul, my body:—1 *Thess.* v. 23.

Thou hast created, and thou hast redeemed them, O Lord God of truth.—*Psalm* xxxi. 5.

And, with me, I commend all my friends, and all my possessions; thou, O Lord, hast graciously given them unto thy servant.—*Gen.* xxxiii. 5.

Preserve my down-sitting and mine up-rising (*Psalm* cxxxix. 2.) from this time forth, and even for evermore:—*Psalm* cxxi. 8.

That I may remember thee upon my bed, (*Psalm* lxiii. 6.) and diligently search out my spirit, (*Psalm* lxxvii. 6.) and, when I awake, be still with thee.—*Psalm* cxxxix. 18.

I will both lay me down in peace, and sleep: for thou, Lord, only makest me dwell in safety.—*Psalm* iv. 8.

A PRAYER FOR ALL ESTATES.

BLESS, O Lord,
The world; the earth that we inhabit.
   The church, the kingdom,
   The throne, the altar,
   The council-table, the judgment-seat,
The places of education, and of traffic.

   Bless all
Infants and children;
Striplings and youths;
Men in vigour and maturity;
The aged and infirm.

   Bless
The tempted, the faint-hearted;

The sick, and the prisoner;
The orphan, the widow, and the stranger.

   Bless
All that travel by land or by water,
All women labouring with child,
 And those that give suck;
All who serve in bitter servitude,
All the forsaken, and heavy laden.

PRAYERS
FOR THE HOLY COMMUNION.

1. *Before receiving the Sacrament.*

LORD, I am not worthy nor deserving that thou shouldst come under the sordid roof of the habitation of my soul:—*Matt.* viii. 8.

For it is all desolate and ruinous; neither in me hast thou a fit place, wherein to lay thy head.—*Luke* ix. 58.

But as thou didst vouchsafe to be laid in the stall and manger of brute beasts;—*Luke* ii. 7.

As thou didst not disdain to be received into the house of Simon the leper;—*Matt.* xxvi. 6.

As thou didst not reject the adulteress, a sinner like unto me, when she approached and touched thee, nor abhor her impure and profane lips;—*Luke* vii. 37, 38.

Neither the thief on the cross, when he confessed thee;—*Luke* xxiii. 43.

Even so vouchsafe to admit me also, a bruised, a wretched, and exceeding sinful creature, to a communion and participation in the spotless, holy, quickening, and saving sacrament of thy most blessed body and precious blood.—*Liturgy of St. Chrysostom.*

LOOK down, O Lord our God, from thy holy habitation, and from the throne of glory in thy kingdom, and come and bless us.—*Deut.* xxvi. 15.

O thou who sittest on high with the Father, and here, unseen, art present with us, come down, and sanctify these gifts presented to thee, and those for whom, and those by whom, and the purposes whereunto they are offered.—*Liturgies of St. Chrysost. and St. Basil.*

And grant us to partake of them
> In faith that maketh not ashamed;—*Rom.* v. 5.
>
> In love, without dissimulation:—*Rom.* xii. 9.
>
> To the fulfilment of thy commandments;—*John* xiv. 15.
>
> To the exercise of all the fruits of the Spirit;—*Gal.* v. 22.
>
> To our deliverance from every evil;—*Luke* xi. 4.
>
> To the preservation of soul and body:—1 *Thess.* v. 23.

For a symbol of our fellowship;—*Acts* ii. 42.

For a remembrance of thy dispensation;—*Eph.* iii. 2.

For the shewing of thy death;—1 *Cor.* xi. 26.

For the communion of thy body and blood;—1 *Cor.* x. 16.

For the participation of thy Spirit;—1 *Cor.* xii. 13.

For the remission of our sins ;—*Matt.* xxvi. 28.
For the avoiding of enemies ;—2 *Tim.* iii. 5.
For the quieting of our consciences ;—*Matt.* xi. 29.
For the blotting out of our transgressions ;—*Acts* iii. 19.
For the purging of our spots ;—*Heb.* ix. 14.
For the healing of our souls' infirmities ;—1 *Pet.* ii. 24.
For the renewal of our covenant ;—*Psalm* l. 5.
For the meat of spiritual life ;—*John* vi. 27.
For increase of strengthening grace ;—*Heb.* xiii. 9.
  And of consolation ;—*Luke* ii. 25.
For sorrow unto repentance ;—2 *Cor.* vii. 9.
For the enlightening of our understanding ;—*Luke* xxiv. 31.
For the clothing of humility ;—1 *Pet.* v. 5.
For a seal of our faith ;—2 *Cor.* i. 22.
For the fulness of wisdom ;—*Rom.* xi. 33.
For the bond of love ;—*John* xiii. 35.
For a due accompt of our oblations ;—1 *Cor.* xvi. 1.
For the armour of sufferance ;—1 *Pet.* iv. 1.
For the awakening of gratitude ;—*Ps.* cxvi. 12.
For confidence in prayer ;—*Verse* 13.
For mutual in-dwelling ;—*John* vi. 56.
For a pledge of our resurrection ;—*Verse* 54.

For a fit excuse at the judgment;—*Luke* xiv. 18.

For a testament of our inheritance;—*Luke* xxii. 20.

For a type of our perfection :—*John* xvii. 23.

That we, with all thy saints, who from the beginning have pleased thee, may be made partakers of thy incorruptible and eternal benefits, which thou hast prepared, O Lord, for them that love thee, (1 *Cor.* ii. 9.) in whom thou art glorified for ever.—2 *Thess.* i. 10.

O Lamb of God, that takest away the sins of the world,—*John* i. 29.

Take away mine also, for I am a grievous sinner. —1 *Tim.* i. 15.

We, therefore, O Lord, in the presence of thy sacrament, being mindful

Of the saving passions of thy Christ,

Of his life-bestowing cross,

Of his most precious death,

Of his three days' burial,

Of his resurrection from the dead,

Of his ascension into heaven,

Of his seat at the right hand of thee, his Father,

Of his second advent in glory and in terror,

Beseech thee, O Lord, that we, taking part in thy sacraments with the pure testimony of our conscience, (2 *Cor.* i. 12.) may be incorporated in the blessed body and blood of thy Christ:

And that, worthily receiving them, we may have Christ dwelling in our hearts, (*Eph.* iii. 17.) and become a temple of thy Holy Ghost:—1 *Cor.* vi. 19.

Even so, O Lord our God!

And make not any one of us guilty of these awful and heavenly sacraments, neither sickly in soul or body by an unworthy partaking of them.— 1 *Cor.* xi. 27 ; 30.

But grant us, even to our last and latest breath, worthily to conceive the hope of these thy mysteries

To our $\begin{cases} \text{sanctification,} \\ \text{illumination,} \\ \text{and confirmation;} \end{cases}$

To the relief of the burden of our many sins ;
To the discomfiture of every assault of the devil ;
To the dismissal and removal of our evil habits ;
For the mortification of our passions,
The observance of thy commandments,
The increase of thy heavenly grace,
And the attainment of thy kingdom.

2. *After receiving the Sacrament.*

We have now finished and consummated, O Christ our God, according to our ability, the mystery of thy dispensation.

For we have received the memorial of thy death ;
We have seen the type of thy resurrection ;
We have been filled with thy eternal life ;

We have had delight in thy endearments,
Whereof there is no satiety;
And the enjoyment of which, O Lord God, we pray thee to award to all of us, in the world to come.

THE good Lord pardon every one, that loveth him with his whole heart, and seeketh the Lord God of his fathers, though he be not cleansed according to the purification of the saints.—*2 Chron.* xxx. 18, 19.

SPECIAL DUTIES OF CHRISTIAN PEOPLE.

I. What shall I do that I may inherit eternal life?
 1. Keep the commandments.—*Mark* x. 17, 19.

II. What shall we do?
 2. Repent, and be baptized, every one of you.—*Acts* ii. 37, 38.

III. What must I do to be saved?
 3. Believe on the Lord Jesus Christ.—*Acts* xvi. 30, 31.

IV. What shall we do then?—*Luke* iii. 10; 12; 14.
 4. *To the People.* He that hath two coats, let him impart to him that hath none; and he that hath meat, let him do likewise.—*Verse* 11.
 5. *To the Publicans.* Exact no more than that which is appointed you.—*Verse* 13.
 6. *To the Soldiers.* Do violence to no man, neither accuse any falsely; and be content with your wages.—*Verse* 14.

GRANT us, O God,
Knowledge of thy justice,

For { Fear,
Humility,
Repentance,
Fasting,
Prayer, and
Patience,

As a sacrifice.

Grant us,

Faith in thy mercy,

For { Hope,
Consolation,
Thanksgiving,
Alms,
Hymns, and
Obedience,

As an oblation.

MEDITATION THE FIRST.

On the Day of Judgment.

O FATHER, without beginning,
O only-begotten Son,
O quickening Spirit,
Merciful, compassionate, long-suffering,
Of great pity, of great loving-kindness,
  Who lovest the righteous, and hast compassion on the wicked,
  Pardoning our offences, and granting our petitions;
  O God of the repentant,
  O Saviour of sinners,
I have sinned against thee, O Lord,
  And thus and thus have I done.—*Josh.* vii. 20.
      Alas! Alas!
How have I been enticed of mine own lust!—*James* i. 14.
How have I hated instruction!—*Prov.* v. 12.
  I have neither revered nor dreaded
    Thy incomprehensible splendour,
    Thy awful presence,
    Thy terrible power,
    Thy unerring justice,
    Thy endearing kindness.
I will call therefore, if there be any that will answer me: to which of the holy angels shall I turn?—*Job* v. 1.

O wretched man that I am! who shall deliver me from the body of this death?—*Rom.* vii. 24.

How terrible is thy judgment, O Lord!
    When the thrones are prepared,
    When the angels stand by,
    When mankind are introduced,
    When the books are opened,
    When deeds are scrutinized,
    When thoughts are revealed,
    When hidden things of darkness are brought to light.—1 *Cor.* iv. 5.

What will be my sentence?
    Who will extinguish my flame,
    Who will lighten my darkness,
        Unless thou have pity on me?

Grant me tears, O Lord, as thou lovest man,
    grant me many tears, and grant them now!
For at that day there will be
    An inflexible judge,
    A dreadful tribunal,
    Pleadings without excuse,
    Accusations without denial,
    A bitter recompense,
    Torments interminable,
    Fiends inflexible,
    The yawning gulf of hell,
    The roaring stream of fire,
        Of fire, never to be extinguished;
    A dungeon of darkness,
        Of darkness, where no light can penetrate;

Beds of burning ashes,
A worm that never dieth,
Chains that never part asunder,
Chaos without boundary,
A wall we cannot surmount,
Lamentations unpitied;
> None to help,
> None to defend,
> None to liberate.

But I repent, O Lord, O Lord, I do repent; help thou my impenitence; and more and more continually, pierce, cleave, and bruise my heart.

Behold, Lord, what indignation I have wrought against myself,—2 *Cor.* vii. 11.

By reason of the yearning of my flesh,
> So ignorant,—*Luke* xxiii. 34.
> So foolish,—*Psalm* lxxiii. 22.
> So hurtful,—1 *Tim.* vi. 9.

And so dangerous.—*Isaiah* xxvi. 11.

Behold, how I abhor myself,—*Job* xlii. 6.

By reason of { the foolishness, the baseness, and the disgrace } of my heart's desire;

Worthy only of confusion and reproach.

Behold, how continually my confusion is before me, and the shame of my face hath covered me.—*Psalm* xliv. 15.

> Alas, alas! how long?

Behold, Lord, how I denounce myself
> Worthy of eternal punishment, yea and

Of all the miseries of this world.

Behold me, Lord, condemned by my own judgment;—*Tit.* iii. 11.

Behold, O Lord, and enter not into judgment with thy servant.—*Psalm* cxliii. 2.

And now, Lord, I am humbled under thy mighty hand;—1 *Pet.* v. 6.

Unto thee, O Lord, I bow my knees;—*Eph.* iii. 14.

I fall on my face to the earth.—*Josh.* v. 14.

Let this cup pass from me.—*Matt.* xxvi. 39.

I stretch forth my hands unto thee;—*Psalm* clxiii. 6.

I smite upon my breast;—*Luke* xviii. 13.

I smite upon my thigh.—*Jer.* xxxi. 19.

Out of the depths my soul crieth unto thee;—*Psalm* cxxx. 1.

It thirsteth after thee as a thirsty land,—*Psalm* cxliii. 6.

And so do all my bones,—*Psalm* xxxv. 10.

And all that is within me.—*Psalm* ciii. 1.

O Lord, hear my voice!—*Psalm* lxi. 1.

MEDITATION THE SECOND.

On the Frailty of Human Life.

Have mercy upon me, O Lord, for I am weak;—*Psalm* vi. 2.

Remember how short my time is;—*Psalm* lxxxix. 47.

Remember that I am but flesh; a wind that passeth away, and cometh not again.—*Psalm* lxxviii. 39.

My days are as grass, and as the flower of the field;—*Isaiah* xl. 6.

The wind shall pass over me, and I shall not abide, neither shall I know my place any more.—*Psalm* ciii. 16.

For I am but dust and ashes,—*Gen.* xviii. 27.

> Earth and hay,—*Prov.* xxvii. 25.
>
> Flesh and wind,—*Psalm* lxxviii. 39.
>
> Corruption and the worm;—*Job* xvii. 14.

As a stranger and a sojourner on earth;—*Ps.* xxxix. 12.

> Dwelling in a house of clay;—*Job* iv. 19.
>
> Whose days are few and evil;—*Gen.* xlvii. 9.
>
> A creature of to-day, not of to-morrow;—*Prov.* xxvii. 1.
>
> Of the morning, but that reacheth not till evening;—*Isaiah* xxxviii. 13.
>
> In a body of sin;—*Rom.* vi. 6.
>
> In a world of corruption;—2 *Pet.* i. 4.
>
> Of few days, and full of trouble;—*Job* xiv. 1.

Like a flower, withering while it flourisheth,
> And, as it were a shadow, continuing not.—*Verse* 2.

REMEMBER this, O Lord; forgive, and pardon. —*Psalm* lxxiv. 18.

For what profit is there in my blood, when I go down to the pit?—*Psalm* xxx. 9.

According unto the multitude of thy mercies, —*Psalm* li. 1.

According to the riches of thy grace,—*Eph.* i. 7.

And the superabundant stores of thy compassion; —*Rom.* v. 20.

> By whatever is dear unto thee, or worthy of our remembrance;—*Gen.* xix. 29.
>
> But, above all and beyond all, for thine own sake,—*Dan.* ix. 18.
>
> For thine own sake, O Lord, and for thy Christ's sake,—*John* xiv. 13.

Be merciful, O Lord, to me, the chief of sinners. —1 *Tim.* i. 15.

O my God, let mercy rejoice against judgment over my transgressions.—*James* ii. 13.

O Lord, hear; O Lord, forgive; O Lord, hearken; O Lord, hearken and do; defer not, for thine own sake; defer not, O Lord, my God!— *Dan.* ix. 19.

DAILY PRAYERS AND MEDITATIONS.

PART THE SECOND.

"Dost thou pray? thou communest with thy spouse. Dost thou read? thy spouse communeth with thee."—*St. Jerome.*

"Reading enricheth prayer; by prayer reading is enlightened."—*William of Paris.*

DAILY PRAYERS AND MEDITATIONS.

·SECOND PART.

A GENERAL CONFESSION.

TWO things, O Lord, I recognise in myself: Nature, which thou madest; Sin, which I have added.

I confess that by sin I have deformed nature: but remember that I am but a wind that passeth away and cometh not again (*Ps.* lxxviii. 39.): for of myself I am not able to return from sin.

Up, Lord; take away from me that which I have made; let that which thou hast made abide in me: neither let that perish, which thou hast redeemed with thy precious blood.

Up, Lord; let not my unworthiness destroy that which thy kindness hath redeemed.

O Lord, my God, though I have made myself a malefactor in thy sight, could I make myself to cease to be thy servant?

Though I have cast away mine own innocence, could I also trample down thy mercy?

Though I have committed deeds worthy of condemnation, hast thou also lost the means of my salvation?

Verily, O Lord, my conscience deserveth judgment, but thy mercy outstrippeth all defence.

Spare me, therefore:
For it is not difficult to thy power,
> It is not unbecoming to thy justice,
> It is not unusual to thy mercy,
>> To spare a sinner.

Thou who hast created me,
> Do not destroy me;

Thou who hast redeemed me,
> Do not condemn me.

Thou who hast created me in thy goodness, suffer not thy handy-work to perish by my iniquity.

Acknowledge whatsoever in me is thine, and take away whatsoever in me is mine own.

Let thy unbounded loving-kindness look down upon my misery: let thy universal pity look upon my guilt.

Weak, I betake me to the Omnipotent; wounded, I fly to the Physician.

Keep for me in store the bounty of thy compassion, since thou hast so long withheld the sword of thy wrath.

Blot out the multitude of my offences; renew the abundance of thy mercies.

Though I be defiled and blinded,
> Diseased and even dead,
> Yet thou canst cleanse me,

Thou canst enlighten me,
Thou canst heal me,
Nay, thou canst bring me back to life.
Such as I am, whether I be good, or whether I be evil, I am ever thine.
If thou deny me, if thou despise me,
Who will receive me? who will regard me?
Thou canst forgive, thou canst spare,
Even more than I can sin or offend.

LET not any baneful inclinations work me harm,
Let not any evil habit work my destruction.
But keep me from corrupt and lawless passions,
Keep me from vain, injurious, and impure imaginations,
Keep me from the delusions of malignant spirits,
From pollutions both of mind and body.

MORNING PRAYERS.

O THOU that hearest prayer, unto thee shall all flesh come.—*Psalm* lxv. 2.

Evening, and morning, and at noon, will I pray and cry aloud; and thou shalt hear my voice.—*Psalm* lv. 17.

In the morning will I direct my prayer unto thee; my voice shalt thou hear in the morning.—*Psalm* v. 3.

Let my prayer be set forth in thy sight as incense.—*Psalm* cxli. 2.

I will remember thee in my bed, O Lord, because thou hast been my helper.—*Psalm* lxiii. 7, 8.

I YIELD thee thanks, Almighty Lord and everlasting God, because thou hast vouchsafed to preserve me this night, not according to my deserts, but according to thy sacred mercy.

Grant me, O Lord, so to pass this day in thy sacred service, that the homage of my duty may please thee.

I LIFT up my heart and my hands unto the Lord in heaven.

Behold, as the eyes of servants look unto the hands of their masters, and as the eyes of a maiden unto the hands of her mistress, so our eyes wait upon the Lord our God, until that he have mercy upon us.—*Psalm* cxxiii. 2.

Look thou upon me, and be merciful unto me, as thou usest to do unto those that love thy name. —*Psalm* cxix. 132.

Give thy angels charge over me, to keep me in all my ways.—*Psalm* xci. 11.

Shew me thy ways, and teach me thy paths.— *Psalm* xxv. 4.

Order my steps in thy word, and let not any iniquity have dominion over me.—*Psalm* cxix. 133.

Hold up my goings in thy paths, that my footsteps slip not.—*Psalm* xvii. 5.

Put into my mouth a right and becoming speech, that all my words, and looks, and gestures, and deeds, may be acceptable in thy sight (*Psalm* xix. 14.), and in the sight and hearing of all men.

O God of kindness and love,—*Titus* iii. 4.

Very pitiful and of tender mercy,—*James* v. 11.

Father of mercies,—2 *Cor.* i. 3.

Rich in mercy towards all those who call upon thee ;—*Eph.* ii. 4.

I have sinned against Heaven, and before thee, and am no more worthy to be called thy son ; I am not even worthy to be made one of thy hired servants, no, not the meanest of them all.—*Luke* xv. 18, 19.

But I repent, alas ! I repent; help thou my impenitence :—*Mark* ix. 24.

And, if there be any consolation in thy love, (*Philem.* 7.) I entreat thee by the bowels of thy mercies, (*Phil.* ii. 1.) by the abundance, (*Rom.* v. 17.) by the riches of thy grace, (*Eph.* i. 7.) by the exceeding abundance of thy mercies, (1 *Tim.* i. 14.) by the great love wherewith thou hast loved us, (*Eph.* ii. 4.) be merciful to me a sinner, (*Luke* xviii. 13.) be merciful to me the chief, the most miserable, of sinners.—1 *Tim.* i. 15.

Deep calleth unto deep;—*Psalm* xlii. 2.

The depth of our wretchedness upon the depth of thy mercy.

Where sin hath abounded, may grace much more abound;—*Rom.* v. 20.

Overcome our evil with thy good;—*Rom.* xii. 21.

Let thy mercy rejoice against thy judgment on our offences.—*James* ii. 13.

Nay, so be it, O Lord.

BUT above all things, and before all, I believe that thou art the Christ, the Son of the living God.—*Matt.* xvi. 16.

O thou that camest into the world to save sinners, of whom I am chief (1 *Tim.* i. 15.); save me.

Thou that takest away the sins of the world (*John* i. 29.); take away my sins.

Thou that camest to seek and to save that which

was lost (*Luke* xix. 10.); suffer not that which thou hast saved to suffer evil.

Free me from the remembrance of evil things, that I record not before the world those things which I have either seen or heard from wicked men, nor ever mention them to others: and that I hold in abhorrence every wicked way.

I have deserved death; yet I still appeal from the tribunal of thy justice unto the throne of thy grace.

A GENERAL SUPPLICATION.

Let us pray:
For the catholic church.
For all the churches throughout the world;
    For their truth, unity, and stability;
    That love may abound and truth flourish, in them all.
For our own church;
    That whatsoever is deficient therein may be supplied,
    And whatsoever is wrong may be corrected;
    That all heresies, schisms, and offences, both public and private, may be removed.
O God, reclaim the wandering,
    Convert the unbelieving,
    Increase the faith of thy church,
    Root out heresies,

Expose our secret, and overthrow our open, enemies.

For the clergy;
That they may rightly divide the word of truth;
—*2 Tim.* ii. 15.
That they may walk circumspectly;—*Eph.* v. 15.
That, teaching others, (*2 Tim.* ii. 2.) they may themselves learn both the way and the truth.—*John* xiv. 6.

For the people;
That they make not themselves over-wise;—*Eccles.* vii. 16.
But be persuaded by reason, and yield to the authority of their superiors.

For the kingdoms of the world;
Their stability and peace.
For our own kingdom, municipality, and city;
That they abide in prosperity and happiness, and be delivered from all peril and disaster.

For the king;
O Lord, save him; O Lord, give him prosperity.
Compass him with the shield of truth and glory;—*Psalm* v. 12.
Speak good things unto his heart, in behalf of thy church and people.

FOR the wisdom of our senators,
  The equity and integrity of our judges,
  The bravery of our troops,
  The moderation and devout simplicity of the people.

FOR our growing youth,
  Whether in colleges or schools;
  That they may increase, as in stature, so in wisdom, and in favour with God and man.—*Luke* ii. 52.

UNTO all, who shew themselves zealous in the cause either of the church or of the poor, render seven-fold into their bosoms.—*Psalm* lxxix. 12.

May their souls dwell at ease, and may their seed inherit the earth.—*Psalm* xxv. 13.

Blessed be they that consider the poor.—*Psalm* xli. 1.

  WE beseech thee, O Lord,
  To recompence all our benefactors with eternal blessings; that in return for the good things they have imparted to us on earth, they may obtain imperishable rewards in heaven.
  To behold, and in thy mercy to relieve, the sorrows of the needy and the captive.
  To restore, in thy kind compassion, the lapses of this fragile flesh, and to strengthen those that fall.

To accept with favour our bounden duty and service.—*Liturgy*.

To raise our minds to heavenly desires.

To cast on us an eye of pity.

To rescue our souls, and the souls of our neighbours, from eternal condemnation.

Finally, to give me grace, that with these, for whom I have prayed, and with those for whom I am by any duty bound to pray, I may be admitted into thy kingdom, there to appear in righteousness, and to be filled with glory.—*Col.* iii. 4.

Hear us, O Lord, we beseech thee.

AN ACT OF THANKSGIVING.

Let all thy works praise thee, O Lord, and let all thy saints bless thee.—*Psalm* cxlv. 10.

It is a good thing to give thanks unto the Lord, and to sing praises unto thy name, O thou Most High;—*Psalm* xcii. 1.

To shew forth thy loving-kindness in the morning, and thy faithfulness every night.—*Verse* 2.

I will extol thee, O God my King, and I will bless thy name for ever and ever.—*Psalm* cxlv. 1.

Every day will I bless thee, and I will praise thy name for ever and ever.—*Verse* 2.

For thou didst call those things which be not, as though they were.—*Rom.* iv. 17.

By thee were all things created, that are in heaven, and that are in earth, visible and invisible.—*Col.* i. 16.

Thou upholdest all things by the word of thy power.—*Heb.* i. 3.

Thou leavest not thyself without witness, in that thou doest good, and givest us rain from heaven, and fruitful seasons, filling our hearts with food and gladness.—*Acts* xiv. 17.

And all thy works continue to this day according to thine ordinances; for they are all thy servants.—*Psalm* cxix. 91.

Moreover, after deliberation held, thou didst form man with thine own hands out of the dust of the ground, and breathe into his nostrils the breath of life:—*Gen.* ii. 7.

With thine own image didst thou honour him;—*Gen.* i. 27.

And unto thine angels didst thou give charge over him;—*Psalm* xci. 11.

And madest him to have dominion over the works of thy hands;—*Psalm* viii. 6.

And didst place him in the paradise of Eden.—*Gen.* ii. 15.

And though he despised thy commandments, thou didst not despise him; but didst open unto him the gate to repentance and life;—*Acts* xi. 18.

>Giving unto him the exceeding great and precious promise of the Saviour's seed.—2 *Pet.* i. 4.   *Gen.* iii. 15.

Thou didst instruct our race,
>By the known attributes of God;
>By the work of the law written in our hearts;
>—*Rom.* ii. 15.

By the offering of sacrifices;
By the oracles of prophets,
By the melody of psalms,
By the wisdom of proverbs,
By the experience of histories.

And when the fulness of the time was come, thou didst send forth thy Son;—*Gal.* iv. 4.

Who took on him the seed of Abraham;—*Heb.* ii. 16.

Who made himself of no reputation, and took upon him the form of a servant;—*Phil.* ii. 7.

Who, made of a woman, made under the law,—*Gal.* iv. 4.

By the offering of his life, manifested obedience to the law, and by the sacrifice of his death took away the curse of the law;—*Gal.* iii. 13.

Redeeming mankind by his death, and quickening them by his resurrection;—*Rom.* iv. 25.

Leaving nothing undone, that ought to have been done;—*Isaiah* v. 4.

That we might be made partakers of the divine nature;—2 *Pet.* i. 4.

Who hath made manifest the savour of his knowledge (2 *Cor.* ii. 14.) through the preaching of his gospel;—2 *Cor.* x. 14.

Bearing witness unto himself by divers signs and wonders;—*Heb.* ii. 4.

By surprising holiness of life;—*Luke* i. 75.

By the exceeding greatness of his power,—*Eph.* i. 19.

Even unto the shedding of blood ;—*Heb.* ix. 22.

By his incredible conversion of the whole world to faith (1 *John* v. 4.) without any aid of force or persuasion.

Furthermore, thou hast made us partakers of the inheritance of the saints, (*Col.* i. 12.) and heirs with them of the same promise.—*Heb.* xi. 9.

Thou hast granted unto thy church, to be the pillar and ground of the truth ;—1 *Tim.* iii. 15.

And that the gates of hell should not prevail against it.—*Matt.* xvi. 18.

Thou hast given unto our church to keep that which is committed to its trust;—1 *Tim.* vi. 20.

To shew us the way of salvation ;—*Acts* xvi. 17.

And to maintain order, stedfastness, and beauty. —*Col.* ii. 5.

Thou hast stablished the throne of thy servant, our king;—2 *Sam.* vii. 13.

Thou hast made peace in our borders, and filled us with the flower of wheat;—*Psalm* cxlvii. 14.

Thou hast strengthened the bars of our gates, and blessed our children within us.—*Verse* 13.

Thine enemies hast thou clothed with shame ;— *Psalm* cxxxii. 18.

But thou hast made us most blessed for ever, and made us exceeding glad with thy countenance. —*Psalm* xxi. 6.

Thou hast informed our princes, and taught our senators wisdom.—*Psalm* cv. 22.

Thou hast given us pastors according to thy heart, which should feed us with knowledge and understanding.—*Jer.* iii. 15.

Thou hast beaten our swords into plough-shares, and our spears into pruning-hooks.—*Isaiah* ii. 4.

For there is no decay, no leading into captivity, and no complaining in our streets.—*Ps.* cxliv. 14.

Thou hast brought me forth into this life; thou hast brought me unto the washing of regeneration, and renewing of the Holy Ghost;—*Tit.* iii. 5.

And made known thy ways unto me.—*Psalm* ciii. 7.

Thou hast winked at my sins, because I should amend;—*Wisd.* xi. 23.

Neither hast thou consumed me because of mine iniquity;—*Isaiah* lxiv. 7.

Waiting that thou mightest have mercy upon me.—*Isaiah* xxx. 18.

Thou hast not suffered my heart to be hardened: —*Mark* viii. 17.

But hast given it over to be pricked,—*Acts* ii. 37.

To remember the days of old,—*Deut.* xxxii. 7.

To feel conscious of former sin.—*Heb.* x. 2.

Thou hast opened to me the gate of hope,—*Psalm* cxviii. 19.

 When I confessed,—1 *John* i. 9.

 And besought thee,—*Acts* xxvi. 3.

By the gift of inspiration,—*John* xx. 22.

And of the keys.—*Matt.* xvi. 19.

Thou hast not cut off, like a weaver, my life,

while I was yet beginning, nor from day to night hast thou made an end of me.—*Isaiah* xxxviii. 12.

Neither hast thou recalled half my days,—*Psalm* lv. 23.

But hast held my soul in life, and suffered not my feet to be moved.—*Psalm* lxvi. 9.

For all these things, O God the Father, I give thanks unto thee always, in the name of our Lord Jesus Christ.—*Ephes.* v. 20.

A DEPRECATION

Against Wrath to come.

O LORD our God, look down from thy habitation in heaven, and from the throne of the glory of thy kingdom.—*Isaiah* lxiii. 15.

Thou who dwellest on high, and humblest thyself to behold the things that are in earth;—*Psalm* cxiii. 5, 6.

Look, Lord, and destroy not; but rather deliver us from evil.—*Matt.* vi. 13.

From all the terrors of the life to come,
From thy wrath, and from everlasting damnation,
—*Liturgy*.
   Good Lord, deliver us.
From all reproach, assault, and infamy,
From deceitful tongues and lying lips,
From all the snares of the wicked,
   Good Lord, deliver us.
From all our enemies,
 Visible and invisible,

Corporeal and spiritual,
>Good Lord, deliver us.

From sin, error, and concupiscence,
From the crafts and assaults of the devil,— *Liturgy.*
>Good Lord, deliver us.

From the lust of fornication,
From the pride of vain-glory,
From every uncleanness of mind and body,
>Good Lord, deliver us.

From anger and ill-will,
From infectious imaginations,
And from blindness of heart,—*Liturgy.*
>Good Lord, deliver us.

O THOU, who spakest to the destroying angel, saying, It is enough, stay now thine hand;—1 *Chr.* xxi. 15.

>In all our prayers and vows,
>In all our difficulties and dangers,
>In all our weaknesses and necessities,
>In all our trials and tribulations,

Repel the greediness of appetite, and grant us the virtue of abstinence;

Dismiss the spirit of incontinence, and grant us the love of chastity;

Extinguish the affections of the world, and grant us meekness of heart;

Restrain headlong wrath, and kindle in us gentleness of disposition;

Remove the sorrows of life, and increase our
  joyfulness of spirit;
Check the boastings of knowledge, and supply
  us with tenderness of conscience.
  Grant us strength of faith,
  Grant us security of hope,
  Grant us assurance of protection,
And contempt for the vanities of the world.

GRANT me the power and opportunity of doing good, that, before the day of my departure hence, I may atchieve at least some useful work, the fruit of which may abide: so that I may be able to appear in righteousness, and be filled with glory.—*Col.* iii. 4.

Thou who didst add unto the days of Hezekiah fifteen years (2 *Kings* xx. 6.), vouchsafe unto me so long, and so long only, a term of life, that I may be able to bewail my sins.

And grant unto me a happy end, which is the greatest blessing of all; a happy and a holy end of this life, a glorious and a joyful resurrection.

OF the fruits of the earth and fulness thereof (*Deut.* xxxiii. 16.) abundantly bless our provision.—*Psalm* cxxxii. 15.

Make peace in our borders, and fill us with the flour of wheat.—*Psalm* cxlvii. 14.

Satisfy our poor with bread.—*Psalm* cxxxii. 15.

Strengthen the bars of our gates, and bless our children within us.—*Psalm* cxlvii. 13.

Clothe our enemies with shame.—*Ps.* cxxxii. 18.

BLESS us with temperature of seasons;
Yield to us the fruits of the earth;
Drive away carnal desires;
Restore health to the sick, and strength to the fallen.
> Grant a serviceable journey and safe harbourage to those that travel by land and water.
> Grant, to the afflicted, joy;
>> To the oppressed, relief;
>> To the captive, liberty.

Vouchsafe unto us all, health of mind and purity of body.

AN EVENING SACRIFICE.

MAY I remember thy name, O Lord, in the night, and may I keep thy law:—*Psalm* cxix. 55.

Let my prayer ascend unto thee at evening, (*Psalm* lxxxviii. 1, 2.) and let thy mercy descend on me:—*Psalm* xxxiii. 22.

Who givest songs in the night;—*Job* xxxv. 10.

Who makest the outgoings of the morning and evening to rejoice;—*Psalm* lxv. 8.

Who givest thy beloved the sleep of health.—*Psalm* cxxvii. 2.

THE HOROLGY;

OR, DIAL OF PRAYER.

THOU who hast put the times and the seasons in thine own power;—*Acts* i. 7.

Grant that we may pray unto thee in a fit and acceptable time:—*Psalm* lxix. 13.

And save us.

Thou who, for us men and for our salvation, wast born at midnight;—*Luke* ii. 8.

Grant that we may be daily regenerate by the renewing of the Holy Ghost;—*Tit.* iii. 5.

Until Christ be formed in us (*Gal.* iv. 19.) unto a perfect man:—*Eph.* iv. 13.

And save us.

Thou who, very early in the morning, at the

rising of the sun, didst rise from the dead;—*Mark* xvi. 2.

Raise us up daily unto newness of life;—*Rom.* vi. 4.

Suggesting to us the means of repentance, which thou best knowest;—*Rom.* ii. 4.

And save us.

Thou who, at the third hour, didst send down the Holy Ghost into thine apostles;—*Acts* ii. 15.

Take not away that same Spirit from us;—*Psalm* li. 11.

But renew it daily in our hearts;—*Verse* 10;

And save us.

Thou who, at the sixth hour, and on the sixth day, didst nail the sins of the world to the same cross with thy self;—*Matt.* xxvii. 45.

Blot out the hand-writing of our offences that is against us, and take it out of the way;—*Col.* ii. 14.

And save us.

Thou who, at the sixth hour, didst let down from heaven to earth a great sheet, the type of thy church;—*Acts* x. 9; 11.

Receive us, sinners of the Gentiles, into it;—*Gal.* ii. 15.

And receive us up together with it into heaven;—*Acts* x. 16.

And save us.

Thou who, at the seventh hour, didst ordain

that the ruler's son should be released of his fever;
—*John* iv. 52.

If any fever or disease adhere to our souls, remove that also from us;

And save us.

Thou who, at the ninth hour, (*Mark* xv. 34.) for us sinners and for our sins, didst taste death; —*Heb.* ii. 9.

Mortify our members which are upon the earth.—*Col.* iii. 5.

And whatsoever is contrary unto thy will; —*Lev.* xxvi. 21.

And save us.

Thou who hast ordained that the ninth hour should be the hour of prayer;—*Acts* iii. I.

Hear us when we call upon thee at the hour of prayer, and make us to obtain our prayers and wishes;

And save us.

Thou who, at the tenth hour, didst choose that thine apostle, having found thy Son, should exclaim with great joy, We have found the Messias; —*John* i. 39; 41.

Grant that we may also in like manner find the same Messias, and, having found him, may in like manner rejoice;

And save us.

Thou who, even at the eleventh hour of the day, didst deign, with promise of reward, to send into thy vineyard those who were standing all the day idle;—*Matt.* xx. 6, 7.

Shew us the same favour, and though late, even as at the eleventh hour, yet vouchsafe to receive us when we turn to thee;

And save us.

Thou who, at the solemn hour of supper, didst institute the mysteries of thy body and blood;—*Matt.* xxvi. 20.

Make us ever mindful and partakers of the same (1 *Cor.* xi. 26.), and that never unto damnation (*Verse* 29.), but unto remission of sin, and to our obtaining the inheritance of the New Testament;

And save us.

Thou who, when even was come, wouldst be taken from the cross, and interred in a sepulchre; —*Mark* xv. 42.

Take away from us, and bury with thee in thy sepulchre (*Rom.* vi. 4.), our sins, covering with good works the evil we have committed;

And save us.

Thou who, late at evening, didst by thy breathing confer on thy disciples the power both of remitting and of retaining sins;—*John* xx. 19; 22, 23.

Make us partakers of that power, but to remission only, O Lord, and not to retention;

And save us.

Thou who, at midnight, didst rouse thy prophet David, (*Psalm* cxix. 62.) and thy apostle Paul, to praise thee;—*Acts* xvi. 25.

Grant us also songs in the night;—*Job* xxxv. 10.

And to remember thee upon our beds;— *Psalm* lxiii. 6.

And save us.

Thou who, at midnight, didst with thine own mouth announce the coming of the bridegroom;— *Matt.* xxv. 6.

Grant that in our ears that cry may ever sound, The bridegroom cometh, that we be never unprepared to meet him;

And save us.

Thou who, by the crowing of the cock, didst admonish thine apostle, and make him return unto repentance;—*Luke* xxii. 60, 61.

Grant that, at the same warning, we may also do the like; that is, go out and weep bitterly for the sins we have committed against thee;— *Verse* 62.

And save us.

Thou who hast foretold that thou wilt come to judgment in a day when we look not for thee, and at an hour when we are not aware;—*Luke* xii. 46.

Make us to be every day and every hour prepared to attend thy coming;

And save us.

Thou who sendest out the light, (*Ps.* xliii. 3.) and preparest the morning, (*Psalm* lxxiv. 16.) and makest the sun to rise on the good and on the evil;—*Matt.* v. 45.

Enlighten the blindness of our hearts by the knowledge of truth;—*Eph.* i. 18; *and* iv. 18.

Lift up the light of thy countenance upon us;
—*Psalm* iv. 6.

That in thy light we may see light, (*Psalm* xxxvi. 9.) even in the light of thy grace the light of glory;

And save us.

Thou who givest food to all flesh;—*Ps.* cxxxvi. 25.

Who feedest the young ravens that call upon thee;—*Psalm* cxlvii. 9.

Who hast nourished us from our youth;—*Psalm* lxxi. 5.

Fill our hearts with food and gladness;—*Acts* xiv. 17.

Stablish our hearts with thy grace;—*Heb.* xiii. 9.

And save us.

Thou who makest evening the end of day (*Ps.* civ. 20.), to bring into our remembrance the evening of life.

Grant that we may ever bear in mind that our life passeth over us like the day;—*Psalm* cii. 11.

Grant that we may always remember the days of darkness, for they are many (*Eccles.* xi. 8.); and that the night cometh, when no man can work;—*John* ix. 4.

Grant that we may work while it is day, that we be not cast into outer darkness;—*Matt.* xxv. 30.

Grant that we may ever cry unto thee, Abide with us, for it is toward evening, and the day of our life is now far spent;—*Luke* xxiv. 29.

And save us.

APPEALS TO THE DEITY.

I. ON THE PART OF GOD.

The Nature of God.

BECAUSE the Lord is merciful and gracious, slow to anger and plenteous in mercy.—*Psalm* ciii. 8.

He will not always chide, neither will he keep his anger for ever.—*Verse* 9.

He hath not dealt with us after our sins, nor rewarded us according to our iniquities.—*Verse* 10.

For as the heaven is high above the earth, so great is his mercy toward them that fear him.—*Verse* 11.

As far as the east is from the west, so far hath he removed our transgressions from us.—*Verse* 12.

Like as a father pitieth his children, so the Lord pitieth them that fear him.—*Verse* 13.

For the Lord is good, and ready to forgive, and plenteous in mercy unto all them that call upon him.—*Psalm* lxxxvi. 5.

The Lord is good to all, and his tender mercies are over all his works.—*Psalm* cxlv. 9.

For he delighteth in mercy :—*Micah* vii. 18.

He is the Father of mercies :—2 *Cor.* i. 3.

He is mercy.—*Psalm* lix. 17.

To him forgiveness is common and peculiar;—*Psalm* cxxx. 4.

To him punishment is strange and unfrequent.—*Isaiah* xxviii. 21.

The Name of God.

LET the power of the Lord be great, according as he hath spoken, saying;

The Lord is long-suffering, and of great mercy, forgiving iniquity and transgression.—*Numb.* xiv. 17, 18

The Name of the Father.

I ASCEND unto my Father and your Father.—*John* xx. 17.

The Father of the prodigal son.—*Luke* xv. 20.

And what wilt thou do unto thy great name?—*Josh.* vii. 9.

The Name of the Son.

THE Lamb, after the type.—Behold the Lamb of God.—*John* i. 29.

The Redeemer.—I know that my Redeemer liveth.—*Job* xix. 25.

The Saviour.—We know that this is indeed the Saviour of the world.—*John* iv. 42.

The Mediator.—One Mediator between God and men.—1 *Tim.* ii. 5.

The Advocate.—We have an Advocate with the Father.—1 *John* ii. 1.

The Intercessor.—He ever liveth to make intercession for us.—*Heb.* vii. 25.

The High-priest.—We have a great High-priest, that is passed into the Heavens, JESUS the Son of God.—*Heb.* iv. 14.

The Name of the Holy Ghost.

THE Dove, in the type.—He saw the Spirit of God descending like a Dove.—*Matt.* iii. 16.

Unction or Anointing.—As the Anointing teacheth you of all things.—1 *John* ii. 27.

The Comforter.—If I go not away, the Comforter will not come unto you.—*John* xvi. 7.

The Promises of God.

REMEMBER thy word unto thy servant, upon which thou hast caused me to hope.—*Psalm* cxix. 49.

God, that cannot lie, hath promised.—*Tit.* i. 2.

He hath confirmed it by an oath.—*Heb.* vi. 17.

His faith the unbelief of men shall not make without effect.—*Rom.* iii. 3.

If we believe not, yet he abideth faithful; he cannot deny himself.—2 *Tim.* ii. 13.

The Performances of God.

OUR fathers trusted in thee; they trusted, and thou didst deliver them.—*Psalm* xxii. 4.

Remember, O Lord, thy tender mercies, and thy loving-kindnesses: for they have been ever of old. —*Psalm* xxv. 6.

Lord, where are thy former loving-kindnesses?
—*Psalm* lxxxix. 49.

Hear me, O children, ye generations of men, and know, that never did any trust in the Lord, and was confounded; or abide in his fear, and was forsaken.—*Ecclus.* ii. 10.

II. ON OUR OWN PART. BY OUR RELATION TO GOD.

The Work of his Hands.

FORSAKE not the work of thine own hands.—*Ps.* cxxxviii. 8.

We are the clay and thou our Potter, and we all are the works of thy hands.—*Isaiah* lxiv. 8.

Thou abhorrest nothing which thou hast made.—*Wisd.* xi. 24.

The Image of his Countenance.
That he efface it not.

LET us make man in our image, after our own likeness.—*Gen.* i. 26.

Who is renewed in knowledge after the image of him that created him.—*Col.* iii. 10.

Despise not thine own likeness.—*Gen.* v. 1.

The Price of his Blood.
That he disparage it not.

YE are bought with a great price:—1 *Cor.* vi. 20.

With the precious blood of the Lamb, without blemish and without spot.—1 *Pet.* i. 19.

The Application of his Name to us.

WE are called by thy name.—*Jer.* xiv. 9.

Thy people are called by thy name.—*Dan.* ix. 19.

A chosen vessel to bear thy name.—*Acts* ix. 15.

Members of the Body of Christ.
That he cut us not off.

YE are the body of Christ, and members in particular.—1 *Cor.* xii. 27.

Know ye not that your bodies are the members of Christ?—1 *Cor.* vi. 15.

Know ye not that your members are the temple of the Holy Ghost, which is in you?—*Verse* 19.

Our Subjection to Christ.

I AM thine; save me.—*Psalm* cxix. 94.

Behold, O Lord, I am thy servant; I am thy servant, and the son of thine handmaid.—*Psalm* cxvi. 16.

We are all thy people.—*Isaiah* lxiv. 9.

Carest thou not that we perish? yea, thou carest.—*Mark* iv. 38.

We are unprofitable servants, yet thy servants.—*Luke* xvii. 10.

We are prodigal sons, still thy sons.—*Luke* xv. 30.

III. ON OUR OWN PART. IN RELATION TO OURSELVES.

The Infirmity of our Nature.

For I am weak.—*Psalm* vi. 2.

Remember how short my time is.—*Psalm* lxxxix. 47.

And he remembered that they were but flesh; a wind that passeth away, and cometh not again.—*Psalm* lxxviii. 39.

For he knoweth our frame; he remembereth that we are dust.—*Psalm* ciii. 14.

As for man, his days are as grass; as a flower of the field, so he flourisheth.—*Verse* 15.

For the wind passeth over it, and it is gone; and the place thereof shall know it no more.—*Verse* 16.

The Wretchedness of our Condition.

We are brought very low.—*Psalm* lxxix. 8.

He regarded their affliction, when he heard their cry.—*Psalm* cvi. 44.

IV. ON OUR PART. AS REGARDS OUR DUTY.

As Penitents.

A broken and a contrite heart, O God, thou wilt not despise.—*Psalm* li. 17.

For I will declare mine iniquity; I will be sorry for my sin.—*Psalm* xxxviii. 18.

As Suppliants.

For I cry unto thee daily.—*Psalm* lxxxvi. 3.

How long wilt thou be angry against the prayer of thy servant?—*Psalm* lxxx. 4.

I forgave thee all the debt, because thou desiredst me.—*Matt.* xviii. 32.

Because we forgive others.

Forgive, and ye shall be forgiven.—*Luke* vi. 37.

And when ye stand praying, forgive, if ye have ought against any; that your Father also, which is in heaven, may forgive you your trespasses. —*Mark* xi. 25.

But if ye do not forgive, neither will your Father, which is in heaven, forgive your trespasses. —*Verse* 26.

Because we purpose henceforward to amend.

My soul breaketh for the longing that it hath to thy judgments at all times.—*Psalm* cxix. 20.

My hands will I lift up unto thy commandments, which I have loved.—*Verse* 48.

I made haste, and delayed not to keep thy commandments.—*Verse* 60.

Who desire to fear thy name.—*Neh.* i. 11.

That servant, which prepared not himself, neither did according to his Lord's will, shall be beaten. —*Luke* xii. 47.

V. IN CONSIDERATION OF EVIL TO ENSUE FROM OUR PUNISHMENT.

No Advantage gained.

WHAT profit is there in my blood, when I go down to the pit? shall the dust praise thee; shall it declare thy truth?—*Psalm* xxx. 9.

For in death no man remembereth thee; and who will give thee thanks in the pit?—*Psalm* vi. 5.

Wilt thou shew wonders to the dead? or shall the dead arise and praise thee?—*Ps.* lxxxviii. 10.

Shall thy loving-kindness be declared in the grave? or thy faithfulness in destruction?—*Verse* 11.

Shall thy wonders be known in the dark? and thy righteousness in the land of forgetfulness?—*Verse* 12.

For the grave cannot praise thee; death cannot celebrate thee: they that go down into the pit, cannot hope for thy truth.—*Isaiah* xxxviii. 18.

The living, the living, he shall praise thee.—*Verse* 19.

The Purpose of our Creation defeated.

WHEREFORE hast thou made all men in vain?—*Psalm* lxxxix. 47.

Enter not into judgment with thy servant, for in thy sight shall no man living be justified.—*Psalm* cxliii. 2.

If thou, Lord, shouldest mark iniquities, O Lord, who shall stand?—*Psalm* cxxx. 3.

If he will contend with him, he cannot answer him one of a thousand—*Job* ix. 3.

The Triumph of our Enemies.

GIVE not thine heritage to reproach, that the heathen should rule over them: wherefore should they say among the people, Where is their God?—*Joel* ii. 17.

Remember this, that the enemy hath reproached, O Lord, and that the foolish people have blasphemed thy name.—*Psalm* lxxxiv. 18.

The tumult of those that rise up against thee, increaseth continually.—*Verse* 23.

The Egyptians will say, For mischief did he bring them out, to slay them in the mountains, and consume them from the face of the earth.—*Exod.* xxxii. 12.

The Canaanites will say, Because he was not able to bring the people into the land which he sware unto them, therefore he hath slain them in the wilderness.—*Numb.* xiv. 16.

VI. IN CONSIDERATION OF GOOD TO ENSUE FROM OUR PARDON.

The Glory of his Name.

FOR the glory of thy name, O Lord, deliver us:—*Psalm* lxxix. 9.

So we thy people will give thee thanks for ever; we will shew forth thy praise to all generations.—*Verse* 13.

The Conversion of Others.

I WILL teach transgressors thy ways, and sinners shall be converted unto thee.—*Psalm* li. 13.

An Example to the World.

HOWBEIT for this cause I obtained mercy, that in me first Jesus Christ might shew forth all long-suffering, for a pattern to them which should hereafter believe on him to life everlasting.—1 *Tim.* i. 16.

An Evidence of the Godhead.

I AM he that blotteth out transgressions for mine own sake.—*Isaiah* xliii. 25.

Hearken and do; defer not for thine own sake.—*Dan.* ix. 19.

Him hath God set forth to be a propitiation.—*Rom.* iii. 25.

Look upon the face of thine Anointed.—*Psalm* lxxxiv. 9.

Turn not away the face of thine Anointed.—*Psalm* cxxxii. 10.

Regard to his own Family.

HAVE mercy on me, thou Son of David.—*Matt.* xv. 22.

And David said unto Shimei, Thou shalt not die; and he sware unto him.—2 *Sam.* xix. 23.

Fulfilment of his Office.

THE Spirit of God is upon me, because he hath anointed me; the Lord hath sent me to preach good tidings unto the meek, and to heal the brokenhearted.—*Isaiah* lxi. 1. *Luke* iv. 18.

I am come to call sinners.—*Matt.* ix. 13.

God sent his Son, that the world through him might be saved.—*John* iii. 17.

A CONFESSION OF PRAISE TO GOD.

For the Excellence of his Majesty.

O FATHER, glorify thou me with thine own self with the glory which I had with thee before the world was.—*John* xvii. 5.

Melchizedek was priest of the most high God. —*Gen.* xiv. 18.

For his Exaltation.

FOR there is a higher than the highest.—*Eccles.* v. 8.

For his Eternity.

HE called on the name of the everlasting God.— *Gen.* xxi. 33.

For his Omnipresence.

Do not I fill heaven and earth? saith the Lord.— *Jer.* xxiii. 24.

Whither shall I go from thy Spirit? or whither

shall I flee from thy presence ? If I ascend up into heaven, thou art there ; if I go down to hell, thou art there also.—*Psalm* cxxxix. 7, 8, &c.

For his Omniscience.

THOU knowest all things.—*John* xxi. 17.

For thou only knowest the hearts of all the children of men.—1 *Kings* viii. 39.

For his Omnipotence.

WITH God nothing is impossible.—*Luke* i. 37.

I am the Almighty God.—*Gen.* xvii. 1.

For the Depth of his Wisdom.

O THE depth of the riches both of the wisdom and knowledge of God! How unsearchable are his judgments, and his ways past finding out!—*Rom.* xi. 33.

For his unshaken Truth.

THE truth of the Lord endureth for ever.—*Psalm* cxvii. 2.

Heaven and earth shall pass away, but my words shall not pass away.—*Matt.* xxiv. 35.

For his consummate Justice.

HIS justice abideth for ever.—*Psalm* cxvii. 2.

He is the Fountain, the Sea, the Abyss of Mercy.

DEEP calleth unto deep.—*Psalm* xlii. 7.

Kind to overlook, to wink.

I BESEECH you by the meekness and gentleness of Christ.—*2 Cor.* x. 1.

I will not destroy it for ten's sake.—*Gen.* xviii. 32.

Thou passest by transgression.—*Micah* vii. 18.

The times of this ignorance God winked at.—*Acts* xvii. 30.

Patient, Long-suffering.

DESPISEST thou the riches of his forbearance and long-suffering?—*Rom.* ii. 4.

Pitiful.

HE, being full of compassion, forgave their iniquity, and destroyed them not.—*Psalm* lxxviii. 39.

Unwilling to punish.

O EPHRAIM, what shall I do unto thee? O Judah, what shall I do unto thee?—*Hosea* vi. 4.

Many times didst thou deliver them; many years didst thou forbear them:—*Neh.* ix. 28; 30.

And for thy great mercies' sake thou didst not utterly consume them.—*Verse* 31.

He hath not dealt with us after our sins, nor rewarded us according to our iniquities.—*Psalm* ciii. 10.

She hath received of the Lord's hand double for all her sins.—*Isaiah* xl. 2.

Like as a father pitieth his children, so the Lord pitieth them that fear him.—*Psalm* ciii. 13.

Sympathizing with our Infirmities.

HE repenteth him of the evil.—*Joel* ii. 13.

Soon relaxing from his Anger.

HE will not always chide, neither will he keep his anger for ever.—*Psalm* ciii. 9.

Prone to Pardon.

I FORGAVE thee all the debt, because thou desiredst me.—*Matt.* xviii. 32.

To Reconciliation.

RECONCILING the world unto himself, not imputing their trespasses unto the world.—*2 Cor.* v. 19.

To Propitiation.

BRING forth quickly the best robe, and put it on him; and put a ring on his hand, and shoes on his feet; and bring hither the fatted calf, and kill it.—*Luke* xv. 22, 23, &c.

Benevolent.

FOR he is kind unto the unthankful and to the evil.—*Luke* vi. 35.

Bountiful.

BESTOWING for the labour of an hour the payment of a day.—*Matt.* xx. 9.

To-day shalt thou be with me in paradise.—
Luke xxiii. 43.

GIVING sight unto the blind.
Loosing the bound.
Clothing the naked.
Raising the fallen.
Upholding the infirm.
Healing the sick.
Collecting the dispersed.
Feeding the living.
Strengthening the hungry.
Raising the dead to life.
Debasing the proud.
Exalting the humble.
Redeeming the captive.
Helping all in the hour of need.

WHO is like unto thee, O Lord, among the gods? who is like thee, glorious in holiness, fearful in praises, doing wonders?—*Exod.* xv. 11.

THE PASSION OF OUR LORD.

A Supplication for Pardon.

O, BY thy sufferings, which here unworthy I recount, deliver my soul from the sufferings of hell.

The Seven last Words of Christ.

1. FATHER, forgive them.—*Luke* xxiii. 34.
2. Woman, behold thy son.—*John* xix. 26.
3. To-day shalt thou be with me in paradise.—*Luke* xxiii. 43.
4. Eli, Eli, lama sabachthani?—*Matt.* xxvii. 46.
5. I thirst.—*John* xix. 28.
6. It is finished.—*Verse* 30.
7. Father, into thy hands I commend my spirit.—*Luke* xxiii. 46.

THOU who didst submit thy glorious head to be wounded, pardon thereby whatever by the wilfulness of my head I have done amiss.

Thou who didst suffer thy hands to be perforated, pardon thereby whatsoever I have done amiss by unlawful touch, by unlawful execution.

Thou who didst allow thy precious side to be pierced, pardon thereby whatsoever I have done amiss, in the heat of passion, by unlawful imaginations.

Thou who didst permit thy blessed feet to be nailed down, pardon thereby whatsoever I have done amiss in the progress of my footsteps, ever swift to evil.

Thou who didst give thy whole body to be stretched upon the cross, pardon thereby whatsoever sins I have committed by the co-operation of all my members.

AND I, O Lord, I also am wounded in my soul.—*Psalm* cix. 21.

Behold the number, the length, the breadth, the depth of my wounds, from my head to the sole of my foot:—*Isaiah* i. 6.

And, by thine own wounds, heal mine, O Lord.—*Isaiah* liii. 5.

Introductory Petitions.

LET my prayer come before thee.—*Ps.* lxxxviii. 2.
 Let it come up to thee.—2 *Chron.* xxx. 27.
 Let it come in unto thee.—*Jonah* ii. 7.
 Let it be set forth before thee.—*Psalm* cxli. 2.
 Let it obtain favour in thy sight.—*Esther* ii. 17.
 Let it come near before thee.—*Ps.* cxix. 169.

I PRAY also that it return not unto me void;—*Isaiah* lv. 11.
 But be willing, as thou art able,
  To hear my voice;—*Psalm* cxix. 149.
  To incline thine ear;—*Dan.* ix. 18.
  To hearken and consider;—*Psalm* xlv. 10.
  To understand;—*Psalm* cxxxix. 2.
  To listen;—*Isaiah* xlix. 1.
  To hearken and do.—*Dan.* ix. 19.

Deprecation.

Put not thy servant away in anger.—*Ps.* xxvii. 9.
　Turn not away thine eyes.—*Cant.* vi. 5.
　Hide not thy face.—*Job* xiii. 24.
　Cover not thyself with a cloud.—*Lam.* iii. 44.
　Shut not up thine ear.—*Verse* 8.
　Forsake me not.—*Psalm* xxvii. 9.
　Abandon me not for ever.—*Psalm* xiii. 1.
　Despise me not.—*Psalm* eii. 17.
　Be not silent to me.—*Psalm* xxviii. 1.
　Sleep not.—*Matt.* viii. 24.
　Stand not afar off.—*Psalm* x. 1.
　Cast me not off.—*Psalm* xliv. 23.
　Take not away thy loving-kindness from me.—*Psalm* lxxxix. 33.
　Forswear not thy truth.—*Verse* 49.
　Rebuke me not in thine anger.—*Psalm* vi. 1.
　Chasten me not in thy displeasure.—*Psalm* xxxviii. 1.
　Remove me not from before thy face.—*Jer.* xxxii. 31.
　Reject me not from among thy children.—*Ps.* lxxxii. 6.
　Take not thy Holy Spirit from me.—*Ps.* li. 11.
　Forget me not for ever.—*Psalm* lxxiv. 19.
　Be not wroth with me very sore.—*Is.* lxiv. 9.
　Deliver me not into the hand of mischief.—*Ps.* xxvi. 10.

Bruise me not.—*Isaiah* liii. 10.
Delay not to turn again.—*Hab.* ii. 3.
Gather not my soul with sinners.—*Ps.* xxvi. 9.

If for a time by thy permission we endure the strength of the enemy, yet let us not be swallowed up by their rapacious jaws.

Let the lion be subdued by the gentle sheep; the turbulent spirit by the feeble flesh.

A CONFESSION OF SIN.

I HAVE SINNED.—2 *Sam.* xii. 13.

Surely, Lord, I also am one of them;. for my life bewrayeth me.—*Matt.* xxvi. 73.

I confess unto thee, because, if I were willing, I am not able to hide any thing from thee, O Lord.—*Ezek.* xxviii. 3.

Who can bring a clean thing out of an unclean?—*Job* xiv. 4.

I am a sinner by my birth; a transgressor from the womb.—*Isaiah* xlviii. 8.

In sin did my mother conceive me;—*Ps.* li. 5.
A root of bitterness;—*Heb.* xii. 15.
A shoot of the wild olive-tree.—*Rom.* xi. 17.

I HAVE sinned, I have committed iniquity, I have done wickedly before thee.—*Psalm* cvi. 6.

I have wrought wickedness in transgressing thy covenant.—*Deut.* xvii. 2.

I have cast away thy law.—*Isaiah* v. 24.

I have refused instruction.—*Prov.* xv. 32.

I have vexed thy Spirit.—*Isaiah* lxiii. 10.

I have walked after mine own devices.—*Jer.* xviii. 12.

I have proceeded from evil to evil.—*Jer.* ix. 3.

I have neither feared thee,—*Jer.* xliv. 10.

Nor turned back;—*Luke* xv. 18.

Not even when called,—*Jer.* vii. 13.

Not even when stricken.—*Jer.* v. 3. *Prov.* xxiii. 35.

But I have become hardened;—*Heb.* iii. 13.

I have provoked thee;—1 *Kings* xvi. 33. *Ps.* cvi. 33.

And all these things thou hast seen,—*Lament.* iii. 60.

And kept silence.—*Psalm* l. 2.

Let not thine anger come upon me, but let thy grace, I pray, pervade me.

Have mercy on me now, and at the hour of death.

Let not the sinfulness of my flesh bring me to condemnation, but let thy compassion for my weakness effect my pardon.

Rest to the soul.

Sin yet lieth at the door.—*Gen.* iv. 7.

I would not destroy it for ten's sake.—*Gen.* xviii. 32.

God will provide himself on the mountain.—*Gen.* xxii. 8.

The Lord, the Lord God, merciful and gracious, long-suffering, and abundant in goodness and truth, keeping mercy for thousands, forgiving iniquity, and transgression, and sin.—*Exod.* xxxiv. 6, 7.

They shall be afflicted, until they confess;—*Lev.* xxvi. 40.

But when they humble themselves, and acknowledge me,—*Verse* 41.

Then will I remember my covenant.—*Verse* 42.

When evil things are come upon thee, and, led by thy penitence of heart, thou shalt return unto God, he will have compassion on thee, and bless thee, and will circumcise thine heart to love the Lord.—*Deut.* xxx. 1, 2, 3; 6.

Why art thou cast down, O my soul, and why art thou disquieted within me? Hope thou in God, for I shall yet praise him, the help of my countenance, and my God.—*Psalm* xlii. 5.

Return unto thy rest, O my soul, for the Lord will reward thee.—*Psalm* cxvi. 7.

Call to Remembrance.

REMEMBER thy words unto thy servant, upon which thou hast caused me to hope.—*Psalm* cxix. 49.

Uphold me according to thy words, that I may live, and let me not be ashamed of my hope.—*Verse* 116.

He will not always chide, neither will he keep his anger for ever.—*Psalm* ciii. 9.

He will not deal with us after our sins, nor reward us according to our iniquities.—*Verse* 10.

So gracious was he, and so merciful to our sins, that he would not destroy us.—2 *Kings* xiii. 23.

He remembered that we are but flesh, a wind that passeth away, and cometh not again.—*Psalm* lxxviii. 39.

The Triumph of Mercy.

COME now, and let us reason together, saith the Lord; though your sins be as scarlet, they shall be as white as snow; though they be red like crimson, they shall be white as wool.—*Isaiah* i. 18.

In returning and bewailing shalt thou be saved. —*Isaiah* xxx. 15.

The Lord waiteth that he may be gracious unto you.—*Verse* 18.

A bruised reed shall he not break, and smoking flax shall he not quench.—*Isaiah* xlii. 3. *Matt.* xii. 20.

I am he that blotteth out thy transgressions for mine own sake, and will not remember thy sins.— *Isaiah* xliii. 25.

I blot out, as a thick cloud, thy transgressions, and, as a cloud, thy sins: return unto me, and I will redeem thee.—*Isaiah* xliv. 22.

Even to your old age I am he, and even to your

hoar hairs will I carry you; I have made, and I will bear; even I will carry, and will deliver you.—*Isaiah* xlvi. 4.

Surely he hath borne our griefs, and carried our sorrows.—*Isaiah* liii. 4.

He was wounded for our transgressions, he was bruised for our iniquities; the chastisement of our peace was upon him; and with his stripes we are healed.—*Verse* 5.

All we like sheep have gone astray; we have turned every one to his own way; and the Lord hath laid on him the iniquity of us all.—*Verse* 6.

And it shall come to pass that before they call, I will answer; and while they are yet speaking, I will bear.—*Isaiah* lxv. 24.

Have I any pleasure at all that the wicked should die? and not that he should return from his ways and live?—*Ezek.* xviii. 23.

Repent, and turn yourselves from all your transgressions; so iniquity shall not be your ruin.—*Verse* 30.

As I live, I have no pleasure in the death of the wicked, but that the wicked turn from his way and live: turn ye, turn ye from your evil ways; for why will ye die, O house of Israel?—*Ezek.* xxxiii. 11.

The wickedness of the wicked shall not harm him in the day that he turneth from his wickedness. —*Verse* 12.

And if the wicked turn from his wickedness,

and do that which is lawful and right, he shall live thereby.—*Verse* 19.

Let the wicked forsake his way, and the unrighteous man his thoughts, and let him return unto the Lord, and he will have mercy upon him; and to our God, for he will abundantly pardon.—*Isaiah* lv. 7.

AN ACT OF INTERCESSION.

O GOD, thou knowest my foolishness, and my sins are not hid from thee.—*Psalm* lxix. 5.

I acknowledge my transgressions, and my sin is ever before me.—*Psalm* li. 3.

I cover not my transgression, as Adam.—*Job* xxxi. 33.

I incline not my heart to words of wickedness, to frame excuses for my sins.—*Psalm* cxli. 4.

I acknowledge my sin unto thee;—*Ps.* xxxii. 5.

And all that is within me, (*Psalm* ciii. 1.) and all my bones, say:—*Psalm* xxxv. 10.

I have sinned, I have sinned against thee, O Lord;—*Psalm* cvi. 6.

I have gone astray like a lost sheep;—1 *Peter* ii. 25.

I have been froward, as a bullock unaccustomed to the yoke.—*Jer.* xxxi. 18.

I have returned, as a dog to his vomit;—*Prov.* xxvi. 11.

As the sow that was washed to her wallowing in the mire.—2 *Peter* ii. 22.

I give glory to thee, O Lord, and confess; I have sinned against thee, and thus and thus have I done.—*Josh.* vii. 19, 20.

Let not the water-flood overflow me, neither let the deep swallow me up, and let not the pit shut her mouth upon me.—*Psalm* lxix. 15.

Lord, all my desire is before thee, and my groaning is not hid from thee.—*Psalm* xxxviii. 9.

Thou knowest, O Lord, that I say the truth in Christ, and lie not, my conscience also bearing me witness in the Holy Ghost:—*Rom.* ix. 1.

That I am sorrowful and grieved in heart, that I have so sinned against thee:

That I am angry with myself, because my sorrow is not greater:

That I pray to thee

    For a contrite heart;—*Psalm* li. 17.

    For groanings which cannot be uttered;—*Rom.* viii. 26.

    For tears of blood.—*Luke* xxii. 44.

Woe unto me for the desolation of my soul,—*Isaiah* xxiv. 6.

    For the hardness of my heart,—*Rom.* ii. 5.

    For the dryness of mine eyes.—*Jer.* ix. 1.

    BEHOLD, LORD,

Fearfulness and trembling are come upon me, and the fear of death hath overwhelmed me.—*Psalm* lv. 5.

What fear, what terror, what dismay, what

agony must I behold at the day of final judgment!

What confusion will then confound me! by what darkness shall I be then encompassed!

BEHOLD, LORD,

I pronounce myself a culprit, and worthy and deserving of eternal wrath, besides the many troubles of this life.

I have deserved death from thee, O Lord, for thou art just;

Yet I appeal to thee, O Lord, for thou art merciful;

I appeal from the throne of thy judgment to the footstool of thy grace.

Admit this appeal, O Lord; if thou admit it not, we perish.

And carest thou not, O Lord, that we perish?—*Mark* iv. 38.

Thou who willest have all men to be saved;—1 *Tim.* ii. 4.

Thou who art not willing that any should perish.—2 *Peter* iii. 9.

As for me, I am not worthy of the least of all thy mercies.—*Gen.* xxxii. 10.

I am not worthy to be made as one of thy hired servants; no, not the lowest of them.—*Luke* xv. 19.

I am not worthy to eat of the crumbs, which fall from thy table.—*Matt.* xv. 27.

I am not worthy to touch the hem of thy garment.—*Matt.* ix. 20.

But, O, by thy great mercy, by the multitude of thy mercies:—*Lament.* iii. 32.

For thy name's sake, for the glory of thy name;—*Psalm* lxxix. 9.

Be merciful to my sin, for it is great; yea, it is very great.—*Psalm* xxv. 10.

GRANT me the grace of thy Holy Spirit, O God, to thank with perpetual remembrance thy Word and only Son;

In his conception and nativity, as the cleanser of our nature;—*Eph.* ii. 3.

In his passion, cross, and death, as the liberator of our bodies;—*Gal.* v. 3.

In his descent and resurrection after death, as our avenger over hell;—1 *Cor.* xv. 55.

In his ascension, as our fore-runner;—*Heb.* vi. 20.

In his seat at thy right hand, as our advocate;—1 *John* ii. 1.

In his second coming, as the renewer of our faith.—*Heb.* xii. 2.

Who opposeth himself

To ABADDON, the destroyer (*Rev.* ix. 11.), as JESUS the Saviour;

To Satan the adversary, as our Mediator;

To our calumniator } the Devil, as our
To our accuser } Advocate;

To our task-master, as our Redeemer.

THAT Christ himself may be formed in us (*Gal.* iv. 19.) let us be conformed to his image.—*Rom.* viii. 29.

When I wax cold in prayer, and destitute of any grace or heavenly consolation, let me call to mind, O Lord, thy seat above, thy sojourn upon earth, and thy intercession with the Father.

When I grow warm with evil passion or concupiscence, let me not forget thy terrible and solemn tribunal, and let the voice of the last trumpet sound without ceasing in mine ears.

THAT, for thy Christ's sake, I may receive of thee, Anointing Father, thy unction (1 *John* ii. 20.), thy saving grace (*Psalm* lxvii. 2.), the unspeakable gift of thy Holy Ghost,—2 *Cor.* ix. 15.

>   In salutary compunction,
>   In pure knowledge,
>   In fervent prayer,
>   In diffusion of charity,
>   In attestation of the seal
>   And of the pledge;

Let me never quench the Spirit;—1 *Thess.* v. 19.
Nor strive against him;—*Jer.* l. 24.
Nor grieve him;—*Eph.* iv. 30.
Nor offend him.—*Acts* vii. 51.

THAT in thy church we may be called,
That in thy catholic church we may be living members in will and wish;

That in thy holy church we may be partakers in the fellowship of devout men and things, of pious prayers and liturgies, to the belief of remission of our sins, (*Acts* x. 43.) and to the hope of resurrection from the dead unto life eternal;—*Titus* iii. 7.

O Lord, increase our faith,—*Luke* xvii. 5.
    As a grain of mustard seed;—*Ver.* 6.
    Make it not a dead faith;—*James* ii. 20.
    Not for a season;—*John* v. 35.
    Not hypocritical:—*Isaiah* x. 6.
    But faith which worketh by love;—*Gal.* v. 6.
Faith, manifested by works;—*James* ii. 18.
Faith, subservient to virtue;—2 *Pet.* i. 5.
Faith, that overcometh the world;—1 *John* v. 4.
Faith, most holy.—*Jude*, 20.

O GOD of truth, and Prince of peace, let there be peace and truth in our days; let the multitude of them that believe be of one heart and of one soul.—*Acts* iv. 32.

O thou who breakest not the bruised reed, who quenchest not the smoking flax;—*Isaiah* xlii. 3. *Matt.* xii. 20.

Strengthen those that stand in truth and grace, and raise up them that fall in heresies or sins.—*Liturgy.*

I beseech thee, O Lord, by thy great mercy, to remove thine anger from this city and this house; for we have sinned against thee:

To comfort this place, and the whole land, by assuaging justice with mercy.

GRANT that I may love in return those who love me, though unknown to me:

Grant that I may point out to them the mercy of God in my prayers: and bring them, together with me, into thy heavenly kingdom.

AN ACT OF PRAISE.

BLESSED are the people that know the joyful sound; they shall walk, O Lord, in the light of thy countenance.—*Psalm* lxxxix. 15.

In thy name, O Lord, shall they rejoice all the day; and in thy righteousness shall they be exalted.—*Verse* 16.

My mouth shall speak the praise of the Lord; and let all flesh bless his holy name for ever and ever.—*Ps.* cxlv. 21.

Magnify the Lord with me, and let us exalt his name together.—*Psalm* xxxiv. 3.

Come and hearken unto me, all ye that fear God, and I will tell you what he hath done for my soul.—*Psalm* lxvi. 16.

Be thou exalted, O God, above the heavens, and thy glory above all the earth.—*Psalm* cviii. 5.

I will praise thee, O Lord, with my whole heart, in the assembly of the upright, and in the congregation.—*Ps.* cxi. 1.

Open my mouth, (*Psalm* lxxviii. 2.) that I may praise thy name; let me find time to praise thee; and in the sight of angels will I sing unto thee.—*Psalm* lvii. 9.

Accept the praises which I desire to sing unto

thee, unworthy sinner as I am, in truth unworthy, yet praises of devotion and gratitude to thee.

Thou art worthy to receive, O Lord God.—*Rev.* iv. 11.

Thou art my God, and I will praise thee; thou art my God, I will exalt thee.—*Psalm* cxviii. 28.

I will sing unto the Lord as long as I live; I will sing praise to my God while I have my being. —*Psalm* civ. 33.

Glory to God in the highest, on earth peace, good will towards men.—*Luke* ii. 14.

Glory, and honour, and praise, and blessing, and thanksgiving, and wisdom, and virtue, and riches, and power, and might, and holiness, and salvation be unto our God, that liveth for ever, that sitteth upon the throne, and unto the Lamb slain. Hallelujah. Amen.—*Rev.* v. 12, 13. *and* xix. 1.

Hosanna in the highest! Blessed is he that cometh in the name of the Lord.—*Matt.* xxi. 9.

It would rather become me, O Lord, a sinner, an impenitent sinner, and so utterly undeserving, to lie prostrate in thy presence, and with weeping and groaning to ask pardon for my sins, than with my polluted lips to praise thee.

Nevertheless, I put my trust in thy inherent goodness, and say:

Blessed art thou, O God, who hast created and brought me into this life, and so disposed of me that I should be

A living soul, and not a senseless creature;

A man, and not a brute beast;
Civilized, not barbarous;
Free-born, not a slave;
Legitimate, not spurious;
Of honest parentage, not of base or ignominious;
Endowed with reason, not foolish;
Perfect in senses, neither blind nor deaf;
Perfect in limbs, neither halt nor maimed;
Brought up, not exposed;
Trained to learning, not to mechanical arts;
A Christian, not a Pagan;
Preserved from dangers and disgrace;
In days of peace, not in storms of war;
Of sufficient estate, compelled neither to flatter nor to borrow;
Delivered from innumerable transgressions,
And endowed with the gifts of grace, of nature, and of fortune.

O THOU, who, according to thy abundant mercy, hast begotten us again unto a lively hope by the resurrection of Jesus Christ from the dead, to an inheritance incorruptible and undefiled, and that fadeth not away, reserved in heaven for us;—1 *Pet.* i. 3, 4.

Thou, who hast blessed me with all spiritual blessings in heavenly places in Christ;—*Eph.* i. 3.

Thou, who hast comforted me in all my tribulation, since, as the sufferings of Christ have abounded in me, so my consolation also aboundeth by Christ;—2 *Cor.* i. 4, 5.

Thee, O God of my fathers, I thank and praise, for thou hast given me in some measure wisdom and might, and hast made known unto me what I desired of thee, and declared the matter unto me. —*Dan.* ii. 23.

Protestation of Gratitude.

O LORD, I am not worthy of the least of all thy mercies, and of all the truth which thou hast shewed unto thy servant.—*Gen.* xxxii. 10.

And what can I say more unto thee? for thou, O Lord my God, knowest thy servant.—2 *Sam.* vii. 20.

What am I, O Lord, what is thy servant, and what is thy servant's house, that thou shouldest look upon such a dead dog as I am?—2 *Sam.* ix. 8.

Wherefore hast thou loved me thus long?— *John* xiii. 1.

What shall I render unto the Lord for all his benefits toward me?—*Psalm* cxvi. 12.

What thanks can we render to God again, for all the joy wherewith we joy before him?—1 *Thess.* iii. 9.

THOU who hast ordained, O Lord, that on this holy day, and at this hour, I should lift up my soul and praise thee, and offer thee the glory due unto thee;

Accept, O Lord, thyself this spiritual sacrifice of my soul; and receiving it unto thyself at thy spiritual altar, vouchsafe in turn to send me the grace of thy most holy Spirit.

Visit me in thy goodness; pardon all my sin, voluntary as well as involuntary; deliver me from eternal punishment, and from all the sorrows of this world.

Turn my meditations unto godliness; sanctify my spirit, my mind, and my body; and grant that I may adore thee and please thee in piety and holiness of life to the last hour of my existence.

Now unto him that is able to do exceeding abundantly above all that we ask or think, according to the power that worketh in us;

Unto him be glory in the church by Christ Jesus throughout all ages, world without end.—*Eph.* iii. 20, 21.

My soul shall be satisfied as with marrow and fatness; and my mouth shall praise thee with joyful lips.—*Psalm* lxiii. 5.

THE LORD'S PRAYER, PARAPHRASED.

Our Father which art in heaven,
1. Hallowed be thy name;
2. Thy kingdom come,
3. Thy will be done, as in heaven, so in earth;
4. Give us this day our daily bread;
5. And forgive us our debts, as we forgive our debtors;
6. And lead us not into temptation,
7. But deliver us from evil;
   For thine is the kingdom, the power, and the glory, for ever and ever. Amen.—*Matt.* vi. 9 *to* 13. *Luke* xi. 2 *to* 4.

1.

1. May we learn to call upon thy name.
2. Be thou our protector, and our exceeding great reward.—*Gen.* xv. 1.
3. Whatever command hath proceeded from thy mouth, may we never pretend to speak either good or evil against it.
4. Give us bread for sustenance, and raiment for clothing.—1 *Tim.* vi. 8.
5. Forgive now the sin and iniquity of thy servants.
6. And, O Lord, let us not ruminate over-anxiously in our hearts all the day long.
7. Neither let evils overtake us.

II.

1. BLESSED be thy name from this time forth, and for evermore.—*Psalm* cxiii. 2.
2. For the frowardness of the people let not hypocrites rule over us.—*Job* xxxiv. 30.
3. Be it done, O Lord, as it seemeth fit to thee.—*Luke* i. 38.
4. Let not the thistle grow instead of wheat, nor the cockle instead of barley.—*Job* xxxi. 40.
5. I have sinned: what shall I do unto thee, thou Preserver of men?—*Job* vii. 20.
6. I will make a covenant with my senses, that I may not think upon evil.—*Job* xxxi. 1.
7. Deliver me out of six troubles; yea, in seven let no evil touch me.—*Job* v. 19.

III.

1. HOLINESS to the Lord.—*Exod.* xxviii. 36.
2. May we be to thee a royal priesthood.—1 *Pet.* ii. 9.
3. In thy countenance we will go in and out.
4. Let us place our life not in bread alone, but in every word that proceedeth out of thy mouth.—*Matt.* iv. 4.
5. Take away our transgressions, iniquities, and sins.
6. Send us nothing that may tempt, nothing that may embitter, our hearts.
7. Deliver us, O Lord, from the destroying angel, and from every deadly visitation.

IV.

1. FROM the rising of the sun unto the going down of the same, thy name be praised.—*Psalm* cxiii. 3.
2. Be thou our refuge and our portion in the land of the living.—*Psalm* cxlii. 5.
3. Teach us to do thy will, for thou art our God; thy good Spirit lead us into the land of uprightness.—*Psalm* cxliii. 10.
4. The eyes of all wait upon thee, O Lord, and thou givest them their meat in due season: thou openest thine hand, and fillest all things living with plenteousness.—*Ps.* cxlv. 15, 16.
5. Have mercy upon us, O God, after thy great goodness; and according to the multitude of thy mercies, do away our offences.—*Psalm* li. 1.
6. Let not the enemy prevail against us, neither let the son of wickedness approach to hurt us.—*Psalm* lxxxix. 23.
7. Let not calamities come upon us, neither let the scourge approach our tents.

V.

1. LET thy name be a fenced city to us, that we may hasten to exalt it.
2. By thee kings do reign; their hearts are in thy hand, as the rivers of waters, to turn them whithersoever thou wilt. (*Prov.* xxi. 1.) Turn them unto good, O Lord.
3. Let there not be many thoughts in our hearts;

but let thy counsel, O Lord, abide, and be perfected.
4. Two things have I required of thee; deny me not them before I die: give me neither poverty nor riches, but allow me what is necessary and sufficient.—*Prov.* xxx. 7, 8.
5. Who can say with confidence, I am clean from sin? (*Prov.* xx. 9.) Be merciful to thy servants who have sinned against thee, and heal their souls.
6. Keep my path from all occasion of Sin; let me not approach the gates of her house.
7. Send not the cruel angel to us, but let every evil thing be removed far away from our homes.

VI.

1. LET not thy name be blasphemed among the Gentiles through us.—*Rom.* ii. 24.
2. Let every nation and kingdom perish, that will not serve thee, and let them be utterly wasted. —*Isaiah* lx. 12.
3. Let all thy counsels stand, and let all thy purposes be performed.—*Jer.* li. 29.
4. Give seed to the sower, and bread for nourishment to the eater.—*Isaiah* lv. 10.
5. Be not wroth very sore, neither remember our iniquities for ever: behold, see; we are all thy people.—*Isa.* lxiv. 9.
6. Let us never put the stumbling-block of iniquity before our eyes.—*Ezek.* xiv. 4.

7. Set not thy face against us for evil.—*Ezek.* xv. 7.

VII.

1. HOLY is thy name above every name :—*Phil.* ii. 9.

    In sanctity and reverence to be esteemed by all; by some more than by others; by me more than by most others.

    Yet I have not so esteemed it, neither have I essayed to do it, so far as in me lay.

    Woe is me, wretched that I am, that I have not done it; I freely confess my sin.

    I am grieved in heart, in mind, in soul, in spirit.

    Suppliant I pray for pardon, and for grace, that from this time forward I may so speak, do, and live, as to hallow thy name, O Lord.

    And would that others, after my example, might do the same!

2. May thy kingdom, the great object of my wishes, visit me here in a state of grace, that I may visit it hereafter in a state of glory.

    Here also, by thy favour, may I be of some service in the kingdom of men; that in the kingdom of heaven hereafter I may be admitted to a place, though it be the lowest under the feet of thy saints.

3. May the will of the flesh, and the will of man, depart from me.

    May thy holy, just, and gracious will towards earth be done on earth, by me and all the inhabitants of earth, even as it is in heaven.

4. Give me all things that be needful for my health, peace, and happiness;

Give me the bread of angels unto life eternal.

5. Forgive me all my debts, the vast sum of my debts;

My shameful downfalls, my continual backslidings, my daily wallowings.

With thee is propitiation, with the Lord there is mercy; with God is plenteous redemption, and he shall redeem me from all my iniquities.—*Psalm* cxxx. 7, 8.

And other faults I have committed; though I know them not, yet not less heavy, and perchance heavier; wherein I pray to be enlightened, that I may be able to acknowledge them.

6. And lead me not, suffer me not to be led, suffer me not to enter, into temptation;

Remembering and pitying my weakness, my frailty so frequently betrayed.

7. But deliver me from evil:

From evil in myself and my flesh, and in its deceitfulness;

From evil suggestions of the Devil;

From evil sentences, for most justly and fairly have I deserved them;

From evils of the time to come; spare me there, O Lord, though here thou chastise me with fire and sword;

From evils of the present time; nay, spare me, Lord, here also;

From the incumbrances of the world, and its calamities;

From the oppression of disease, wherewith I am afflicted, and of business, wherein I am entangled;

From evils, past, present, and to come;

From all these things deliver me, O Lord, and keep me as thy servant for ever, even though lower than the lowest.

I BESEECH thee, Lord, by all thy mercy, let thy most just indignation be turned away from me;

For often and grievously, very grievously and very often have I sinned against thee, especially in my late, my last offences:

Yet be it turned away from me and from my parents, from my brothers and sisters, my family and kindred, my friends and neighbours, my country, and all Christian people. Amen.

PRAYERS FOR THE HOUSE OF GOD.

1. *On Entrance into Church.*

LORD, I have loved the habitation of thy house, and the place where thine honour dwelleth.—*Psalm* xxvi. 8.

That I may hear the voice of thy praise, and tell of all thy wondrous works.—*Psalm* xxvi. 7.

One thing have I desired of the Lord, that will I seek after; that I may dwell in the house of the Lord all the days of my life, to behold the beauty of the Lord, and to visit his temple.—*Psalm* xxvii. 4.

My heart said unto thee, I will seek the Lord; I have sought thee and thy face; thy face, O Lord, will I seek.—*Verse* 8.

Open to me the gates of righteousness; I will go into them, and I will praise the Lord.—*Psalm* cxviii, 19.

2. *After Confession.*

O MY Saviour, Christ, my Saviour! Who will grant that I may rather die than offend thee any more? O my Saviour, Christ, my Saviour!

O Lord, let my new course of life declare that a new Spirit is come over me:

For life is new, where penitence is sincere; and confession is true, where penitence is incessant:

By observing a perpetual day of rest from sin,

From its occasion, its contagion, and its danger.

For as repentance destroyeth old offences, so new offences destroy repentance.

3. *On Reading and Preaching the Word.*

OPEN thou mine eyes, that I may behold wondrous things out of thy law.—*Psalm* cxix. 18.

Remove the veil from my heart, O Lord, whilst I read the Scriptures.—*Luke* xxiv. 45.

Blessed art thou, O Lord; teach me thy statutes. —*Psalm* cxix. 12.

Give me the Word, the Word of the Father.—
John i. 1.

Touch mine heart.—*Psalm* xvii. 3.

Lighten the thoughts of my heart.—*Psalm* xxxxiii. 11.

Open my lips, and fill them with thy praises.—
Psalm lxxi. 8.

Be thou, O Lord, in my spirit and in my mouth; in my mouth, that I may rightly and duly announce thy oracles, under the sanctifying influence of thy most holy Spirit.

O thou, who didst send the seraphim with a live coal in the tongs to touch the lips of thy prophet, and take away his sins (*Isai.* vi. 6, 7.); touch my lips also, for I am a sinner; cleanse me from every spot, and make me worthy to proclaim thy oracles.

O Lord, open thou my lips, and my mouth shall shew forth thy praise.—*Psalm* li. 15.

O Lord my God, give me a tongue of understanding, that I may know what I ought to speak (*Col.* iv. 3, 4.); even that which is good to the use of edifying, that it may minister grace unto the hearers.—*Eph.* iv. 29.

May language be given me with the opening of my mouth.—*Ezek.* xxix. 21.

Open my mouth wide, O Lord, and fill it.—*Ps.* lxxxi. 10.

The Draught of Fishes.—*Luke* v. 2—6.

THE world,	the sea;
Mankind,	the fishes;
The church,	the boat;
The preacher,	the fisherman;
The Word,	the net.

My Lord, and my God.—*John* xx. 28.

Blessed are they that have not seen, and yet have believed.—*Verse* 29.

I said, I will confess my transgressions unto the Lord; and thou forgavest my iniquity.—*Psalm* xxxxii. 5.

And if he shall come in the second watch, or come in the third watch, and find them so, blessed are those servants.—*Luke* xii. 38.

PRAYER ON GOING A JOURNEY.

GIVE me, O Lord, a favourable journey this day; and even if thou do not thyself accompany me, yet do not hinder my progress.

Thou who didst conduct the servants of Abraham by the guidance of an angel,—*Gen.* xxiv. 7.

And the wise men of the East by a star;—*Matt.* ii. 9.

Who didst save Peter when he had begun to sink,—*Matt.* xiv. 30.

And Paul, when he suffered shipwreck:—*Acts* xxvii. 44.

Be present with me, O Lord, and order my travel;

Guide me on my way, bring me whither I would go, and bring me back again.

Let God arise, and let his enemies be scattered.—*Psalm* lxviii. 1.

Depart from me, ye evil doers; for I will keep the commandments of my God.—*Psalm* cxix. 115.

ART thou not sorry, O my soul? art thou not humbled and ashamed? art thou not grieved, affrighted, and distressed?

Perform then thy oblations unto God;
> If not seven times a day, like David,—*Psalm* cxix. 164.
>> At least three times a day like Daniel.—*Dan.* vi. 10.
> If not at length like Solomon,—1 *Kings* viii. 22—53.
>> At least with brevity, like the publican.—*Luke* xviii. 13.
> If not all night, like Christ,—*Luke* vi. 12.
>> At least one hour.
> If not on the ground, nor in ashes,
>> At least not in thy bed.
> If not in sackcloth,
>> At least not in purple and fine linen.—*Luke* xvi. 19.
> If not altogether from all,
>> At least from daintiness.
> If not fourfold, like Zaccheus,—*Luke* xix. 8.

> At least with the addition of the fifth part.
> —*Lev.* v. 16.

If not as the rich,
> At least as the poor widow.—*Mark* xii. 42.

If not a half,
> At least a thirtieth part.

If not beyond my power,
> At least to the extent of my power.—2 *Cor.* viii. 3.

THE PRAYER OF ARCHBISHOP BRADWARDINE.

(From his Treatise " De Virtute Causarum," published in 1618.)

THEE, O my God, and thee alone, and for thine own sake alone, I love before all things else. Thee I desire, for thee I long unto the end. Thee only, and for thine own sake, and for nothing but thyself, I still seek always and in all things; from the very bottom of my heart, from my inmost soul; with groaning and lamentation; with constant labour and anxiety.

What, then, wilt thou render unto me in the end? if thou render not thyself to me again, thou renderest me nothing; if thou give not thyself to me, thou givest me nothing; if I find not thee, I find not any thing; thou yieldest me no reward, but affliction more abundant.

For even before I sought thee, I hoped at length

to find thee, and to hold thee fast; and with this delightful hope I sweetly comforted myself in all my troubles. But now, if thou deny thyself to me, whatever else thou givest me, yet, defeated of so great a hope, (and that not for a time, but to eternity,) shall I not for ever faint with love, and pine with faintness, and weep with pining, and despair with weeping, because I must remain for ever empty and unsatisfied? Shall I not inconsolably afflict myself? incessantly murmur? and immoderately be tormented?

Such is not thy will, most good, and kind, and loving God; it in no wise agreeth or comporteth with thy nature. Grant therefore, most gracious God, that I may love thee ever, and seek thee everywhere, above all things, and for thy sake, in this life present, and may at length find thee, and hold thee fast for ever, in the life to come. Grant this, for Jesus Christ his sake. Amen.

AN ACT OF ADORATION.

O GOD the FATHER, of heaven,
  Who didst wonderfully create the world out of nothing;
  Who by thy power dost govern and uphold the heavens and the earth;
  Who didst deliver thine only-begotten Son to death for us:

O GOD the SON, Redeemer of the world,
  Who didst vouchsafe to be incarnate of a virgin;
  Who by thy precious blood hast cleansed us from sin;—1 *John* i. 7.
  Who, having risen from the dead, didst ascend in triumph to heaven:

O GOD the HOLY GHOST, the Comforter,
  Who didst descend upon Jesus under the form of a dove;—*Matt.* iii. 16.
  Who didst sit upon the apostles like tongues of fire;—*Acts* ii. 3.
  Who dost visit and confirm by thy grace the hearts of thy saints:

O HOLY, supreme, everlasting, glorious, and blessed Trinity, ever worthy to be praised, yet ever ineffable;
    O righteous Father,

> O kind Son,
> O gentle Spirit,
> Of majesty inexpressible,
> Of power incomparable,
> Of goodness inestimable,
> Whose work is life,
> Whose love is grace,
> Whose contemplation is glory;
> Unity in Trinity,
> But One Godhead;

I pray to thee, I call upon thee, I bless thee with the whole strength of my heart, now and for ever. Amen.

Thou that art the God of the living, as well as of the dead;—*Matt.* xxii. 32.
> To whom both we belong, whom the present life yet detains in the flesh, and they also, who, having put off the body (*Col.* ii. 11.), have passed into the life to come;
> Grant unto the living mercy and grace;
> Grant unto the dead eternal rest and light;
> Grant unto thy Church truth and peace,
> And unto us sinners penitence and pardon.

A PRAYER FOR DELIVERANCE.

As thou didst deliver our fathers,
> So deliver us also, O Lord.

As thou didst deliver, in the days of old,
> Noah from the flood;

Abraham from Hur of the Chaldæans;
Isaac from immolation on the altar;
Jacob from Laban and Esau;
Joseph from his seducer and his jailor;
Job from his temptations;
Moses from Pharaoh and from stoning;
The children of Israel from the Red Sea, and from the captivity of Babylon;
David from Saul and Goliath,
    From Keilah and Achitophel,
    From Absalom, Doeg, and Seba;
Elias from Jezebel;
Hezekiah from Rabshakeh and the plague;
Esther from Haman;
Joah from Athaliah;
Jeremiah from the pit;
Shadrach, Meshach, and Abednego from the furnace;
Jonas from the whale's belly;
The disciples from the storm;
Peter from the prison of Herod,
Paul from shipwreck, stoning, and the wild beast;
So also deliver us, O Lord, who put our trust in thee.—*Psalm* xvii. 7.

AN ACT OF HOPE.

Be thou exalted, Lord, in thine own strength; so will we sing and praise thy power.—*Ps.* xxi. 13.

Let all thy works praise thee, O Lord, and let thy saints bless thee.—*Psalm* cxlv. 10.

To thee I give thanks: thee I worship, and praise, and bless, and glorify.

Thou art worthy, O Lord God, to receive praises and thanks;—*Rev.* iv. 11.

Whom I, a sinner, am not worthy to invoke, to call by name, or even to contemplate in idea.

O LORD, in thee have I trusted; let me not be confounded for ever.—*Te Deum.*

Thou art my hope from my mother's breasts;—*Psalm* xxii. 9.

Thou art my trust from my youth.—*Ps.* lxxi. 5.

My flesh resteth in hope.—*Acts* ii. 26.

Thy word, in which thou hast given me hope.—*Psalm* cxix. 114.

He shall have hope in the end.—*Jer.* xxxi. 17.

The valley of Achor for a door of hope.—*Hos.* ii. 15.

Hope maketh not ashamed.—*Rom.* v. 5.

By hope we are saved.—*Rom.* viii. 24.

The God of hope fill us.—*Rom.* xv. 13.

Though he slay me, yet will I hope in him.—*Job* xiii. 15.

Who savest those that hope in thee.—*Prov.* xxix. 25.

In thy sacred name have we hoped.—*Ps.* ix. 10.

Under the shadow of thy wings will I make my refuge.—*Psalm* lvii. 1.

Thou, Lord, art my hope; my hope is in thee; thou art the hope of all the ends of the earth.—*Psalm* lxv. 5.

Hope in God;—*Psalm* xliii. 5.
Would that I did so more;
I fear that I do so but little;
Woe is me, that I do not more;
Well were it with me, if I did.

I HOPE and BELIEVE,

With David, to see the goodness of the Lord in the land of the living.—*Psalm* xxvii. 13.

With Paul, that Christ Jesus came into the world to save sinners.—1 *Tim.* i. 15.

With John, that if any man sin, we have an advocate with the Father, Jesus Christ the righteous, and that he is the propitiation for our sins, and for the sins of the whole world.—1 *John* ii. 1, 2.

With Peter, that thou art the Christ, the Son of the living God.—*Matt.* xvi. 16.

With Nathaniel, that thou art the Son of God, the King of Israel.—*John* i. 49.

With the Samaritans, that this is indeed the Christ, the Saviour of the world.—*John* iv. 42.

With Martha, that thou art the Christ, the Son of God, which should come into the world.—*John* xi. 27.

With the Eunuch, that Jesus Christ is the Son of God.—*Acts* viii. 37.

With the assembly of apostles and elders, that through the grace of the Lord Jesus Christ we shall be saved.—*Acts* xv. 11.

With Andrew, that I have found the Messias, which is, being interpreted, the Christ.—*John* i. 41.

WE have believed in Jesus Christ, that we might be justified by the faith of Christ, and not by the works of the law.—*Gal.* ii. 16.

For there is one God, and one mediator between God and men, the man Christ Jesus; who gave himself a ransom for all.—1 *Tim.* ii. 5, 6.

And faith worketh with works, and by works faith is made perfect.—*James* ii. 22.

A DOXOLOGY.

SONGS OF PRAISE.

Of the Heavenly Host.

GLORY to God in the highest, and on earth peace, good will toward men.—*Luke* ii. 14.

Of the Jewish Multitudes.

Hosanna to the Son of David.—*Matt.* xxi. 9.

Blessed is the King of Israel, that cometh in the name of the Lord.—*John* xii. 13.

Blessed be the kingdom of our father David, that cometh in the name of the Lord. Hosanna in the highest.—*Mark* xi. 10.

Of the Disciples.

Peace in heaven, and glory in the highest.—*Luke* xix. 38.

Of the four Beasts.

Holy, holy, holy, Lord God Almighty, which was, and is, and is to come.—*Rev.* iv. 8.

Of the Angels.

Worthy is the Lamb that was slain, to receive power, and riches, and wisdom, and strength, and honour, and glory, and blessing.—*Rev.* v. 12.

Of every Creature.

Blessing, and honour, and glory, and power, be unto him that sitteth upon the throne, and unto the Lamb for ever and ever. Amen.—*Verse* 13.

Of the Witnesses in Heaven.

Salvation to our God, which sitteth upon the throne, and unto the Lamb.—*Rev.* vii. 10.

Of all Angels.

Amen. Blessing, and glory, and wisdom, and thanksgiving, and honour, and power, and might, be unto our God for ever and ever. Amen.—*Ver.* 12.

Of the four-and-twenty Elders.

We bless thee, O God Almighty, who wast, and art, and art to come; for thou hast received great power, and reignest.—*Rev.* xix. 6.

At the Marriage of the Lamb.

Praise our God, all ye his servants, and ye that fear him, both small and great.—*Verse* 5.

Let us be glad, and rejoice, and give honour to him; for the marriage of the Lamb is come.—*Verse* 7.

Blessed are they which are called unto the marriage-supper of the Lamb.—*Verse* 9.

HYMNS.

⁎ The Morning, or Angelic, Hymn, as it is sometimes called, from the commencement having been sung by angels at our Saviour's birth, is ascribed, for the most part, to Telesphorus, about the year of Christ 139; the whole being incorporated into the Liturgy of St. James. By some it is supposed that this composition is alluded to in one of the Dialogues of Lucian, where mention is made of the "ᾠδη πολυώνυμος," or " Hymn with many names ;" and our venerable author thought it not unlikely that the same is designated in the Letters of Pliny, as the song which the Christians used to sing together on stated days at break of morn, in honour of Christ their God.

The Evening Hymn, which is also of remote antiquity, will be found recorded, as well as the preceding, in the " Tractatus de Symbolo Apostolico" of Archbishop Usher.

The Monostrophic on the Crucifixion was written by Thomas Masters, of New College, Oxford, who died in 1643. A Latin Translation was published shortly afterwards by Henry Jacob. In English, it appears among the poems of William Cowley, and again among those of Christopher Pitt.

HYMNS.

MORNING HYMN.

GLORY to God on high, and in earth peace, good will towards men.

We praise thee, we bless thee, we worship thee, we glorify thee, we give thanks to thee for thy great glory, O Lord God, heavenly king, God the Father Almighty.

O Lord, the only-begotten Son, Jesu Christ; O Lord God, Lamb of God, Son of the Father, that takest away the sins of the world, have mercy upon us. Thou that takest away the sins of the world, have mercy upon us. Thou that takest away the sins of the world, receive our prayer. Thou that sittest at the right hand of God the Father, have mercy upon us.

For thou only art holy; thou only art the Lord; thou only, O Christ, with the Holy Ghost, art most high in the glory of God the Father. Amen.

EVENING HYMN.

O CHEERFUL light of the sacred glory of the immortal, heavenly, holy, blessed Father, Jesu Christ.

Having reached the setting of the sun, and beholding the star of evening, we praise the Father, the Son, and the Holy Spirit of God.

Worthy art thou at every hour to be celebrated by holy lips, O Son of God, thou giver of life.

Therefore the world doth glorify thee.

CHRIST CRUCIFIED.

A MONOSTROPHIC.

1.

ENOUGH, enough! thy babbling verse
    No more, vain Muse, prolong;
Henceforth with harp and lute rehearse
    A nobler, holier song;
To Heav'n let loud Hosannas ring
The triumph of our martyr'd King.

2.

Amaz'd before th' abyss I pause
    Of miracles profound,
And, wrapt in Heav'n's mysterious laws,
    A wonder would expound;
A wonder angels cannot scan,—
How God immortal died for man.

3.

Mercy of mercies! Son by Sire
  To foes a hostage giv'n!
Three days a buried corpse, aspire
  In glory back to Heav'n!
Captivity in thraldom led,
And Death by Death discomfited!

4.

These would I sing; but groan and shriek
  Of vengeance and of pain
On Calvary's mount a story speak,—
  The slayer and the slain:
Above the hill look high in air,—
Hang there not three in torment there?

5.

And one, the midst, (nor anger He
  Alone, nor terror shews,)
Outstretch'd upon th' accursed tree,
  His forehead meekly bows;
His bleeding hands and ankles view,
With nails of iron broken through.

6.

Vain, wretched man! behold, and wake!
  With shame repentance blend;
Thy cheek and breast, for sorrow's sake,
  Thy hair and garment rend;
Beat thy hard heart, and learn the bliss
Of anguish deep and dear as this!

7.

Before thee runs the purple flood,—
  No dye of Tyrian wave,—
But gushing deep from wounds of blood,
  The crown of mockery gave;
Or lash'd from every stripe and sore,
The cruel scourge hath furrow'd o'er.

8.

Weep, child of man, insensate, weep,
  The gates of grief set free;
The ground in tears for Jesus steep,
  He drench'd in blood for thee.
For boon like His grudge not in turn
The sacrifice of hearts that mourn.

A MANUAL FOR THE SICK.

"Though the Lord give you the bread of adversity, and the water of affliction, yet shall not thy teachers be removed into a corner any more: but thine eyes shall see thy teachers;

"And thine ears shall hear a word behind thee, saying, This is the way, walk ye in it."—*Isaiah* xxx. 20, 21.

A MANUAL FOR THE SICK.

PREPARATORY ADMONITIONS.

SET thine house in order, for thou shalt die.—2 *Kings* xx. 1. *Isaiah* xxxviii. 1.

Is any sick among you? let him call the priests of the Church, and let them pray over him:

And the prayer of faith shall save the sick, and the Lord shall raise him up; and if he have committed sins, they shall be forgiven him.—*James* v. 14, 15.

INQUIRIES TO BE MADE CONCERNING THE SICK PARTY.

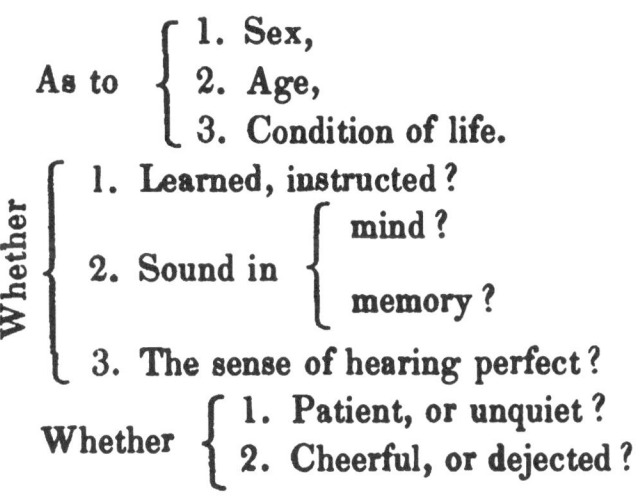

Whether, when in good health, he have found comfort,

In { hearing, reading, repeating particulars?

Whether there be any material point, whereof he ought to be admonished?

Mem. To take occasion out of his own words.

GENERAL CONSIDERATIONS OF THE MORTALITY OF MAN.

WHAT man is he that liveth, and shall not see death?—*Psalm* lxxxix. 48.

It is appointed unto men once to die.—*Heb.* ix. 27.

I am a stranger with thee, and a sojourner, as all my fathers were.—*Psalm* xxxix. 12.

Here have we no continuing city.—*Heb.* xiii. 14.

The night cometh, when no man can work.—*John* ix. 4.

If the tree fall toward the south, or toward the north, in the place where the tree falleth, there it shall be.—*Eccles.* xi. 3.

COMFORTABLE SCRIPTURES TO BE USED TO THE SICK.

THE mountains shall depart, and the hills be removed, but my kindness shall not depart from thee, neither shall the covenant of my peace be removed, saith the Lord that hath mercy on thee.—*Isaiah* liv. 10.

Heaven and earth shall pass away, but my words shall not pass away.—*Matt.* xxiv. 35.

All the promises of God in him are Yea and Amen.—2 *Cor.* i. 20.

Whereby are given unto us exceeding great and precious promises, that by these we might be partakers of the divine nature.—2 *Pet.* i. 4.

I have surely heard Ephraim bemoaning himself thus; Thou hast chastised me, and I was chastised, as a bullock unaccustomed to the yoke: turn thou me, and I shall be turned; for thou art the Lord my God.

Surely, after that I was turned, I repented; and after that I was instructed, I smote upon my thigh; I was ashamed, yea even confounded, because I did bear the reproach of my youth.

Since I spake against him, I do earnestly remember him still: therefore my bowels are troubled for him: I will surely have mercy on him, saith the Lord.—*Jer.* xxxi. 18, 19, 20.

I will visit their transgressions with the rod, and their iniquity with stripes:

Nevertheless, my loving-kindness will I not utterly take from him; nor suffer my truth to fail.—*Psalm* lxxxix. 32, 33.

My son, despise not the chastening of the Lord, neither be weary of his correction:

For whom the Lord loveth he correcteth, even as a father the son, in whom, for all that, he delighteth.—*Prov.* iii. 11, 12.

Behold, happy is the man whom God correcteth; therefore despise not thou the chastening of the Almighty:

For he maketh sore, and bindeth up; he woundeth, and his hands make whole.

He shall deliver thee in six troubles; yea, in seven shall no evil touch thee.—*Job* v. 17, 18, 19.

Forget not the exhortation which speaketh unto you as unto children: My son, despise not thou the chastening of the Lord; nor faint when thou art rebuked of him:

For whom the Lord loveth, he chasteneth; and scourgeth every son whom he receiveth.

If ye endure chastening, God dealeth with you as with sons; for what son is he, whom the father chasteneth not?

But if ye be without chastisement, whereof all are partakers, then are ye bastards, and not sons.

Furthermore, we have had fathers of our flesh, which corrected us, and yet we gave them reverence; shall we not much rather be in subjection unto the Father of spirits, and live?

For they, verily, for a few days, chastened us after their own pleasure; but he for our profit, that we might be partakers of his holiness.

Now, no chastening for the present seemeth to be joyous, but grievous; nevertheless, afterward it yieldeth the peaceable fruit of righteousness unto them which are exercised thereby.

Wherefore, lift up the hands which hang down, and the feeble knees.—*Heb.* xii. 5, 6, 7, 8, 9, 10, 11, 12.

And ye now therefore have sorrow; but I will see you again, and your heart shall rejoice; and your joy no man taketh from you.—*John* xvi. 22.

For a small moment have I forsaken thee, but with great mercies will I gather thee:

In a little wrath I hid my face from thee for a moment, but with everlasting kindness will I have mercy on thee, saith the Lord thy Redeemer.—*Isaiah* liv. 7, 8.

A little while, and ye shall see me.—*John* xvi. 16.

Blessed is the man whom thou chastenest, O Lord, and teachest him out of Thy law;

That Thou mayest give him rest from the days of adversity.—*Psalm* xciv. 12, 13.

But when we are judged, we are chastened of the Lord, that we should not be condemned with the world.—1 *Cor.* xi. 32.

They that sow in tears, shall reap in joy.—*Ps.* cxxvi. 6.

The Lord hath chastened me sore; but he hath not given me over unto death.—*Ps.* cxviii. 18.

My brethren, count it all joy, when ye fall into divers afflictions;

Knowing this, that the trying of your faith worketh patience:

But let patience have her perfect work, that ye may be perfect and entire, wanting nothing.—*James* i. 2, 3, 4.

Blessed are they that mourn; for they shall be comforted.—*Matt.* v. 4.

When I am weak, then am I strong.—2 *Cor.* xii. 10.

The Lord upholdeth all such as fall, and 'lifteth up all those that are down.—*Psalm* cxlv. 14.

He healeth those that are broken in heart, and giveth medicine to heal their sickness.—*Psalm* cxlvii. 3.

My flesh and my heart faileth; but God is the strength of my heart, and my portion for ever.—*Psalm* lxxiii. 25.

Though mine outward man perish, yet let mine inward man be renewed day by day:

O, let this light affliction, which is but for a moment, work for me a far more exceeding and eternal weight of glory!—2 *Cor.* iv. 16, 17.

SEVERAL DUTIES RECOMMENDED TO THE SICK.

I. *Prayer.*

PRAY God if perhaps this may be forgiven thee.—*Acts* viii. 22.

For this shall every one that is godly make his prayer unto thee.—*Psalm* xxxii. 6.

II. *Alms.*

BLESSED is he that considereth the poor and needy.—*Psalm* xli. 1.

By mercy and truth iniquity is purged.—*Prov.* xvi. 6.

Break off thy sins by shewing mercy to the poor.—*Dan* iv. 27.

They shewed the garments which Dorcas had made with her own hands.—*Acts* ix. 39.

(Πέντε τάδε. *These five.*)

III.

Except ye *repent*, ye shall all likewise perish.—*Luke* xiii. 5.

IV.

Without *faith* it is impossible to please God.—*Heb.* xi. 6.

V.

Though I have all faith, and have not *charity*, it profiteth me nothing.—1 *Cor.* xiii. 2, 3.

VI.

We are saved by *hope.*—*Rom.* viii. 24.

VII.

Trust thou in the Lord, and be *doing good.*—*Ps.* xxxvii. 3.

And they shall come forth that have *done good*, unto the resurrection of life.—*John* v. 29.

Make to yourselves friends of the mammon of unrighteousness, that, when ye fail, they may receive you into everlasting habitations.—*Luke* xvi. 9.

Zaccheus stood, and said unto the Lord; Behold, Lord, the half of my goods I give unto the poor, and if I have taken any thing from any man by false accusation, I restore him four-fold.—*Luke* xix. 8.

PROPOSITIONS AND INFERENCES TO BE MADE TO THE SICK.

1. *Concerning the Wisdom and Providence of God, in ordering all Afflictions in general, and this especially.*

You are persuaded that no sickness, or cross, cometh by chance to any one:

But you believe, that it is God who sendeth them, without whose providence they fall not on us.

You acknowledge God to be most wise, and to suffer nothing to befal us, but when it is expedient that it should do so:

And therefore, as God hath sent this his visitation to you at this time, that it is expedient for you thus to be sick.

I KNOW, O Lord, that thy judgments are right, and that thou of very faithfulness hast caused me to be troubled.—*Psalm* cxix. 75.

2. *Concerning the Fatherly Affection and Love of God.*

You know and confess, that unto all, but unto Christians more especially, God beareth the affection of a Father towards his children.

You know also, that a father, whether he dote upon his child, or whether he chasten him, continueth a father in both cases; and loveth him in the one no less than in the other.

Think the same of God, as touching yourself: that, while he gave you good days, he loved you; and that, now he sendeth you some evil, he loveth you also; and would not have sent this evil, but to be a cause unto you of greater good; that, being called home thereby, you might be at peace with him.

BEFORE I was troubled, I went wrong: but now shall I keep thy word.—*Psalm* cxix. 67.

3. *Concerning the Patience and Thankfulness required in the Sick.*

You are not only to take this sickness patiently; (I became dumb, and opened not my mouth; for it was thy doing.—*Psalm* xxxix. 9. It is the Lord, let him do what seemeth him good.—1 *Sam.* iii. 18.)

But even to give him thanks for it, as for a wholesome medicine: (The Lord gave, and the Lord hath taken away; as it pleaseth the Lord, so is it to come to pass; blessed be the name of the Lord.—*Job* i. 21. I will take this cup of salvation, and call upon the name of the Lord.—*Psalm* cxvi. 12.)

Especially considering, that although we, in the time of our health, have forgotten him, yet is he so merciful, that he giveth us not over with the world; but for all we have often grieved his Holy Spirit, and fallen from grace, he visiteth us again, and offereth it afresh unto us;

And that, if it had not been his will to shew mercy by this chastisement, he could, and would, have suddenly taken you away with a quick destruction; and not have given you this time to bethink yourself, and to seek and sue to him for grace.

WHEN I am judged, I am chastened of the Lord, that I should not be condemned with the world.—1 *Cor.* xi. 32.

God, in his mercy, visiteth our offences with the rod.—*Psalm* lxxxix. 32.

It is of the Lord's mercies that we are not suddenly consumed:—*Lament.* iii. 22.

For he giveth us time and space.—*Rev.* ii. 21.

O, tarry thou the Lord's leisure; be strong, and he shall comfort thine heart; and put thou thy trust in the Lord.—*Psalm* xxvii. 16.

O, cast thy burthen upon the Lord, and he shall nourish thee, and shall not suffer the righteous to fall for ever.—*Psalm* lv. 23.

O, put your trust in him alway, ye people: pour out your hearts before him; for God is our hope. —*Psalm* lxii. 8.

He will not alway be chiding, neither keepeth he his anger for ever.—*Psalm* ciii. 9.

In his wrath he will remember mercy.—*Hab.* iii. 2.

Heaviness may endure for a night, but joy cometh in the morning.—*Psalm* xxx. 5.

For a small moment have I forsaken thee, but with great mercies will I gather thee:

In a little wrath I hid my face from thee for a moment; but with everlasting kindness will I have mercy on thee, saith the Lord thy Redeemer.—*Isaiah* liv. 7, 8.

4. *Concerning the Contrition and Repentance of the Sick.*

Do you acknowledge yourself not to have lived so well as you ought to have done? but to have sinned, done amiss, and dealt wickedly?

Do you call to mind the years of your life spent amiss, in the bitterness of your soul?

Do you desire to have your mind illuminated by God, touching those sins you never knew; or which you once knew, but have now forgotten: that you may repent of them?

Do you desire to feel greater sorrow in your soul for your sins committed, than you do? Would you be glad, if you did feel it? And are you grieved that you feel it not; that you are not more grieved?

Is there any special sin, that lieth heavy on your conscience, for which you need, or would require, the benefit of private absolution?

Thou with rebukes dost chasten man for sin, and makest his beauty to consume away, as it were a moth fretting a garment.—*Psalm* xxxix. 12.

There is no health in my flesh, because of thy displeasure: neither is there any rest in my bones, by reason of my sin.—*Psalm* xxxviii. 3.

Lord, be merciful unto me: heal my soul, for I have sinned against thee.—*Psalm* xli. 4.

Lord, I confess my wickedness, and am sorry for my sin.—*Psalm* xxxviii. 18.

I call to mind the mis-spent years of my life, in the bitterness of my soul.—*Isa.* xxxviii. 15.

My misdeeds prevail against me; O, be thou merciful unto my sin.—*Psalm* lxv. 3.

For thy name's sake, O Lord, be merciful unto my sin; for it is great.—*Psalm* xxv. 10.

O, remember not the sins and offences of my youth; but according to thy mercy think thou upon me, O Lord, for thy goodness.—*Verse* 6.

Namely, O Lord, and specially in ......, be merciful unto me.

In this thing the Lord pardon thy servant:—2 *Kings* v. 18.

Lord, lay not this sin to my charge.—*Acts* vii. 60.

If thou, Lord, wilt be extreme to mark what is done amiss, O Lord, who may abide it?—*Psalm* cxxx. 3.

O, enter not into judgment with thy servant: for in thy sight shall no man living be justified.—*Psalm* cxliii. 2.

My confusion is daily before me, and the shame of my face hath covered me.—*Psalm* xliv. 16.

My heart is disquieted within me, and the fear of death is fallen upon me:

Fearfulness and trembling are come upon me, and an horrible dread hath overwhelmed me.—*Psalm* lv. 4, 5.

The Lord is nigh unto them that are of a contrite heart; and will save such as be of a humble spirit.—*Psalm* xxxiv. 18.

A broken and contrite heart, O God, shalt thou not despise.—*Psalm* li. 17.

REPENT you of these your sins?

That is to say,—

Are you purposed to judge yourself for them, if you live?—1 *Cor.* xi. 31.

And to inflict upon yourself punishment for committing them, according as you shall be directed?—*Lev.* v. 18. 2 *Cor.* vii. 11.

Are you resolved, if God send you life hereafter, to amend and live more carefully? and to avoid both those means and occasions, that may provoke you to sin again? and those signs and marks, which testify that you delight in it?

Do you solemnly promise thus much in the presence of God, his grace assisting you?

Do you desire, if God send you health again, to be speedily put in mind thereof?

TURN us then, O God our Saviour, and let thine anger cease from us.—*Psalm* lxxxv. 4.

5. *Concerning the Belief of the Sick.*

BELIEVE you the Christian Creed, or Confession of our most holy faith, once delivered to the saints?

Believe you that you cannot be saved, except you did believe it?

Are you glad in your soul, and do you give God hearty thanks, that in this faith you were born, that in it you have lived, and that you now die in the same?

Do you yourself desire, and do you wish us to desire, at the hands of God, that this faith may not fail you, until the hour, and in the hour, of death?

If your sense fail you, or if the pain of your disease, or weakness, otherwise so work with you, that you shall happen with your tongue to speak ought otherwise than this your faith or religion warranteth; do you renounce all such words as none of yours? and is it your will, that we account of them as not spoken by you?

Is there in your mind any scruple, touching any matter of your faith or religion?

LORD, I believe; help thou mine unbelief.—*Mark* ix. 24.

6. *Concerning the Sick party's Forgiveness of Offenders against him.*

Do you forgive them, that in any manner have offended you, as freely as you would be forgiven at God's hand?

Do you likewise desire of God, that he would forgive them?

Such amends as they are bound to make you, in that they have offended you, are you content also to remit to them?

Are you willing that thus much be shewed them from you, that you have forgiven them freely and fully, and desire God to do the like?

FATHER, forgive them: for they knew not what they did.—*Luke* xxiii. 34.

Lord, lay not these sins to their charge.—*Acts* vii. 60.

7. *Concerning the Sick party's Desire of Forgiveness from those whom he hath offended.*

AND whereas you have yourself lived in the world, it cannot be but some you have offended: do you desire, therefore, that all such as you have offended, would pardon and forgive you?

Do you remember or call to mind any person or persons in particular, whom you have so offended?

Will you that so much be signified to them in your name, that you desire them to forgive you?

Inasmuch as offences against the Seventh Commandment, of begetting children by an act of adultery committed with the wife of another man; and against the Eighth Commandment, of purloining men's goods; and against the Ninth, of touching men's credit or good name; are not by God forgiven, unless restitution be made to the parties wronged: are you ready and willing to restore, and make satisfaction, to such as you have wronged by thrusting in a child begotten by you, to deprive the true children of the party, begotten by him, of a child's part and portion? and to such as you have defrauded of their goods? and to those whom you have any way touched in their good name? and that without any deceit or delay?

Can you call to mind any persons in particular, whom you have so offended?

PRAYERS, AND EXPRESSIONS OF THE SOUL'S AFFIANCE IN GOD.

AND now, Lord, what is my hope? truly my hope is even in thee.—*Psalm* xxxix. 8.

Thou art the hope of all the ends of the earth, and of them that remain in the broad sea.—*Ps.* lxv. 5.

Though he slay me, yet will I trust in him.—*Job* xiii. 15.

Though I walk through the valley of the shadow of death, I will fear no evil.—*Psalm* xxiii. 4.

He knoweth whereof we are made; he remembereth that we are but dust.—*Psalm* ciii. 14.

Consider that we are but flesh; even a wind

that passeth away, and cometh not again.—*Psalm* lxxviii. 40.

O, remember how short my time is: wherefore hast thou made all men for nought?—*Ps.* lxxxix. 46.

Lord, consider my complaint; for I am brought very low.—*Psalm* cxlii. 7.

Let my present misery more prevail to move thy compassion, than my sinful life past to provoke thine indignation.

O Lord, how long wilt thou be angry with thy servant that prayeth?—*Psalm* lxxx. 4.

Behold, I shew the lowliness of a suppliant: shew not thou to me the rigour of a judge.

Let not, I beseech thee, the sentence of the judge press heavy upon him, whom the petition of a suppliant thus humbleth.

O, deliver not thine own inheritance unto the will of thine enemies.—*Psalm* lxxiv. 20.

I am thine; O, save me.—*Psalm* cxix. 94.

I am thine; carest thou not that I perish?—*Mark* iv. 38.

Behold, O Lord, how that I am thy servant, and the son of thine handmaid;—*Psalm* cxvi. 14.

Thy wicked and unprofitable servant; (*Matt.* xviii. 32. *Luke* xvii. 10.) yet thy servant:

Thy lost unnatural child; (*Luke* xv. 24.) yet thy child.

Though I have not shewn to thee the duty or affection of a son, yet do not thou cast from thee the natural kindness and compassion of a father.

A COMMENDATION OF THE SICK TO THE BLESSED TRINITY.

INTO thy hands I commit myself, as unto a faithful Creator.—1 *Pet.* iv. 19.

Receive, O Lord, thine own image, not made by any strange God, but by thyself, the only true and living God.

Forsake not, O Lord, the *work* of thine own hands.—*Psalm* cxxxviii. 8.

Lord, I am *created* in thine own image:—*Gen.* i. 27.

Suffer not, O Lord, suffer not thine own image to be utterly defaced;

But renew it again in righteousness and true holiness.—*Ephes.* iv. 24.

INTO thy hands I commend my spirit; for thou hast *redeemed* me, O Lord, thou God of truth.—*Psalm* xxxi. 6.

Behold, O Lord, I am the *price of thy blood,* of thy most precious blood:—1 *Cor.* vi. 20.

Suffer not so great a price to perish; suffer not that to be cast away, which thou hast bought so dearly.

O Lord, thou camest down from heaven to *redeem* that which was lost:—*Luke* xix. 10.

Suffer not that to be lost, which thou hast *redeemed.*

BEHOLD, O Lord, thou art in the midst of us, and we are called by *thy name;* (*Jer.* xiv. 9.) we are called by *thy name*, (*Dan.* ix. 19.) *Christians.*—*Acts* xi. 26.

For *thy name's* sake, O Lord, be merciful unto our sins.—*Psalm* xxv. 10.

Spare thine own name in us; neither, good Lord, so remember our sins, that, in remembering them, thou forget thine own name.

Lord, we call upon thy name, besides which there is *none other name* under heaven, whereby we can be saved.—*Acts* iv. 12.

Though we be unfaithful, yet thou abidest true; thou canst not deny *thine own name.*—2 *Tim.* ii. 13.

INTO thy hands I commend myself, as to my true and only *Sanctifier.*

Lord, I have been the temple of thy *Holy Spirit.*—1 *Cor.* iii. 16.

Though it hath been polluted through my frailty, yet, O Lord, destroy it not; but dedicate it, hallow it anew, and sanctify it to thyself: yet once again make a feast of dedication in it.

Spare us, good Lord,

$$\text{Spare} \begin{cases} \text{thine own} \begin{cases} \text{handiwork,} \\ \text{image,} \\ \text{name,} \end{cases} \\ \text{The price of thine own} \\ \quad \text{blood in us.} \end{cases}$$

The good Lord pardon every one, that prepareth his heart to seek God, the Lord God of his fathers, although he be not cleansed according to the purification of the sanctuary.—2 *Chron.* xxx. 18, 19.

Behold, Lord, a bruised reed;
>O, break it not:

Behold smoking flax; and yet, O Lord, do not quench it.—*Isaiah* xlii. 3.   *Matt.* xii. 20.

A PROFESSION OF CHRISTIANITY BY THE SICK,

Demonstrated in many special Graces.

LORD, I have never denied thy name, but confessed it ever; and in the confession and invocation of it I desire to spend my last breath, and to depart this life.

O Lord, I have desired to fear thy name.—*Neh.* i. 11.

My soul hath been desirous to long after thy judgments.—*Psalm* cxix. 20.

I do confess my wickedness, and am sorry for my sin.—*Psalm* xxxviii. 18.

Lord, I believe; help thou mine unbelief.—*Mark* ix. 24.

I believe verily to see the goodness of the Lord in the land of the living;—*Psalm* xxvii. 15.

Let me not be disappointed nor ashamed of this my hope.—*Psalm* cxix. 116.

Lord, I freely forgive whomsoever I have aught against, the poor pence or farthings which they owe me.—*Matt.* xviii. 28.

I became dumb, and opened not my mouth at thy chastisement; because it was thy doing, O Lord.—*Psalm* xxxix. 10.

Lord, I seek thee; and thou never failest them that seek thee.—*Psalm* ix. 10.

I come unto thee; and of them that come to thee, thou castest none out.—*John* vi. 37.

Nevertheless, though I am sometime afraid, yet put I my trust in thee.—*Psalm* lvi. 3.

In thee, O Lord, have I put my trust; let me never be put to confusion.—*Ps.* xxxi. 1. *and* lxxi. 1.

HEADS OF COMFORT,

To be administered from the consideration

OF GOD AND CHRIST.

God is

1. A Creator; and so faithful.—1 *Pet.* iv. 19.
2. A Possessor, or Owner.—*Gen.* xiv. 19. *Isaiah* i. 3.

>I am thine;—*Psalm* cxix. 94.

>A part of thy possession.—*Eph.* i. 14.

3. A Redeemer at large.—*Psalm* cxxx. 7.
4. A Redeemer, as of the same flesh and blood.—*Job* xix. 25.

Christ *is*, 1. *a Mediator:*

Between God and us,

>His priesthood and sacrifice.

2. *A Lion:*

Between us and Satan,

>His kingdom and conquest.

3. *A Lamb:*

Between us and sin,

>His innocency.

Between us and our concupiscence,
  His charity.
Between us and the punishment due to our sins,
  The satisfaction of his passion and blood-shedding.
Between us and our conscience, and the judgment of God,
  His advocateship.
Between us and our want of righteousness,
  His absolute and complete obedience.
Between us and our want of title to the eternal reward,
  His merit.
Between us and our want of fervour in praying,
  His intercession.
Between us and our want of sorrow in repenting,
  His agony and bloody sweat.

These $\left\{\begin{array}{l}\text{recount,}\\ \text{shew,}\\ \text{offer,}\\ \text{set between.}\end{array}\right\}$

A COLLECTION OF PRAYERS, CHIEFLY FROM THE PSALTER,

Suitable to the Exigencies of the Sick.

Psalm vii. Verses 1, 2.

O LORD my God, in thee have I put my trust; save me from all them that seek after my soul, and deliver me;

Lest he devour my soul, like a lion, and tear it in pieces, while there is none to help.

Psalm xviii. *Verse* 3.

The sorrows of death compassed me round about; and the overflowings of ungodliness made me afraid.

Psalm cxvi. *Verses* 3, 4.

The snares of death compassed me round about, and the pains of hell gat hold upon me.

I found trouble and heaviness, and I called upon the name of the Lord: O Lord, I beseech thee, deliver my soul.

Psalm xviii. *Verses* 6; 16.

Hear my voice, O Lord, out of thy holy temple: let my complaint come before thee; let it enter even into thine ears.

Send down from on high, and fetch me; take me out of many waters.

Psalm cxvi. *Verses* 5 *to* 7.

Gracious is the Lord, and righteous; yea, our God is merciful.

The Lord preserveth the simple; I am in misery but he will think upon me.

Turn again then unto thy rest, O my soul; for the Lord hath rewarded thee.

Psalm xxii. *Verses* 1 *to* 5; 9 *to* 11; 20, 21.

My God, my God, look upon me; why hast thou forsaken me? and art so far from my health, and from the words of my complaint?

O my God, I cry in the day-time, but thou hearest not; and in the night-season also I have no audience.

Yet thou continuest holy, O thou worship of Israel.

Our fathers hoped in thee; they trusted in thee, and thou didst deliver them.

They called upon thee, and were holpen; they put their trust in thee, and were not confounded.

But thou art he that took me out of my mother's womb; thou wast my hope when I hanged yet upon my mother's breasts.

I have been left unto thee ever since I was born: thou art my God even from my mother's womb.

O, go not far from me, for trouble is hard at hand; and there is none to help me.

Deliver my soul from the sword; my darling from the power of the dog.

Save me from the lion's mouth; deliver me also from among the horns of the unicorns.

Psalm xxv. *Verses* 10; 15 *to* 17; 19.

For thy name's sake, O Lord, be merciful unto my sin; for it is great.

O, turn thee unto me, and have mercy upon me; for I am desolate, and in misery.

The sorrows of my heart are enlarged: O, bring thou me out of my troubles.

Look upon my adversity and misery; and forgive me all my sin.

O, keep my soul, and deliver me : let me not be confounded; for I have put my trust in thee.

Psalm xxviii. *Verses* 1, 2.

Unto thee do I cry, O Lord my strength ; think no scorn of me ; lest, if thou make as though thou hearest not, I become like them that go down into the pit.

Hear the voice of my humble petitions, when I cry unto thee; when I hold up my hands toward the mercy-seat of thy holy temple.

Psalm xxvii. *Verses* 10, 11.

O, hide not thou thy face from me; nor cast thy servant away in displeasure.

Thou hast been my succour : leave me not, neither forsake me, O God of my salvation.

Psalm xl. *Verses* 14 *to* 16; 20, 21.

Withdraw not thou thy mercy from me, O Lord; let thy loving-kindness and thy truth alway preserve me.

For innumerable troubles are come about me ; my sins have taken such hold upon me, that I am not able to look up; yea, they are more in number than the hairs of my head, and my heart hath failed me.

O Lord, let it be thy pleasure to deliver me; make haste, O Lord, to help me.

As for me, though I be poor and needy, yet the Lord careth for me.

Thou art my Helper and Redeemer: make no long tarrying, O my God.

Psalm xxxi. *Verses* 16 *to* 18.

My hope hath been in thee, O Lord; I have said, Thou art my God.

My time is in thy hand; O, deliver me, and be merciful unto me.

Shew thy servant the light of thy countenance; and save me for thy mercy's sake.

Psalm xxxviii. *Verses* 21, 22.

Forsake me not, O Lord my God; be not thou far from me.

Haste thee to help me; O Lord God of my salvation.

Psalm liv. *Verses* 1, 2.

Save me, O God, for thy name's sake; and deliver me in thy strength.

Hear my prayer, O God; and hearken unto the words of my mouth.

Psalm lv. *Verses* 1, 2.

Hear my prayer, O God, and hide not thyself from my petition.

Take heed unto me, and hear me, how I mourn in my prayer, and am vexed.

Psalm lxi. *Verses* 1, 2.

Hear my crying, O God, give ear unto my prayer.

From the ends of the earth will I call upon thee, when my heart is in heaviness.

Psalm lxix. *Verses* 13 *to* 19; 30.

Lord, let me make my prayer unto thee in an acceptable time.

Hear me, O God, in the multitude of thy mercies; even in the truth of thy salvation.

Take me out of the mire, that I sink not: O, let me be delivered from them that seek my soul, and out of the deep waters.

Let not the water-flood drown me, neither let the deep swallow me up; and let not the pit shut her mouth upon me.

Hear me, O Lord, for thy loving-kindness is comfortable; turn thee unto me according to the multitude of thy mercies.

Hide not thy face from thy servant, for I am in trouble: O, haste thee, and hear me.

Draw nigh unto my soul, and save it: O, deliver me.

As for me, when I am poor and in heaviness, thy help, O God, shall lift me up.

Psalm cix. *Verses* 20 *to* 23; 25, 26.

But deal thou with me, O Lord God, according unto thy name; for sweet is thy mercy.

O, deliver me, for I am helpless and poor; and my heart is wounded within me.

I go hence like the shadow that departeth; and am driven away as the grasshopper.

My knees are weak through fasting; my flesh is dried up for want of fatness.

Help me, O Lord my God; O, save me according to thy mercy:

And men shall know how that this is thy hand; and that thou, Lord, hast done it.

Psalm lxxiv. *Verses* 1, 2; 20; 22.

O God, wherefore art thou absent from us so long? why is thy wrath so hot against the sheep of thy pasture?

O, think upon thy congregation, which thou hast purchased and redeemed of old.

O, deliver not the soul of thy turtle-dove unto the multitude of thine enemies; and forget not the distresses of thy servants for ever.

O, let not the simple go away ashamed; but let the poor and needy give praise unto thy name.

Psalm lxxx. *Verses* 3; 7; 19.

Turn us again, O Lord God of Hosts; shew the light of thy countenance, and we shall be whole.

Psalm lxxxv. *Verses* 2 *to* 7.

O, forgive the offences of thy servants, and cover all their sins.

Take away all thy displeasure, and turn thyself from thy wrathful indignation.

Turn us then, O God our Saviour, and let thine anger cease from us.

Wilt thou be displeased at us for ever? and wilt

thou stretch out thy wrath from one generation to another?

Wilt thou not turn again, and quicken us; that thy people may rejoice in thee?

Shew us thy mercy, O Lord: and grant us thy salvation.

Psalm lxx. *Verse* 1.

Haste thee, O God, to deliver me; make haste to help me, O Lord.

Psalm xliv. *Verses* 23 *to* 26.

Up, Lord, why sleepest thou? awake, and be not absent from us for ever.

Wherefore hidest thou thy face, and forgettest our misery and trouble?

For our soul is brought low, even unto the dust: our belly cleaveth unto the ground.

Arise, and help us; and deliver us for thy mercy's sake.

Psalm lxxxvi. *Verses* 1 *to* 7; 15 *to* 17.

Bow down thine ear, O Lord, and hear me: for I am poor and in misery.

Preserve thou my soul, for thou gavest it me: my God, save thy servant, who putteth his trust in thee.

Be merciful unto me, O Lord: for I will call daily upon thee.

Comfort the soul of thy servant: for unto thee O Lord, do I lift up my soul.

For thou, Lord, art good and gracious, and of great mercy unto all them that call upon thee.

Give ear, Lord, unto my prayer: and ponder the voice of my humble desires.

In the time of my trouble I will call upon thee; for thou hearest me.

For thou, O Lord God, art full of compassion and mercy; long-suffering, plenteous in goodness and truth.

O, turn thee then unto me, and have mercy upon me; give thy strength unto thy servant, and help the son of thine handmaid.

Shew some good token upon me for good, that they who love thee may see it, and be glad; because thou, Lord, hast holpen me and comforted me.

Psalm cxlii. *Verses* 1 *to* 7; 9.

I cried unto the Lord with my voice: yea, even unto the Lord did I make my supplication.

I poured out my complaints before him, and shewed him of my trouble.

When my spirit was in heaviness, thou knewest my path.

I looked also upon my right hand, and lo, there was none that could help me.

I had no place to flee unto; and no man was able to relieve my soul.

I cried unto thee, O Lord, and said, Thou art my hope, and my portion in the land of the living.

Consider my complaint, for I am brought very low.

Bring my soul out of prison, that I may give thanks unto thy name; which thing if thou wilt grant me, then shall the righteous resort unto my company.

Psalm cxli. Verse 9.

Mine eyes look unto thee, O Lord God; in thee is my trust: O, cast not out my soul.

Psalm lxxxviii. Verses 1, 2; 9 to 16.

O Lord God of my salvation, I have cried day and night before thee: O, let my prayer enter into thy presence: incline thine ear unto my calling.

For my soul is full of trouble, and my life draweth nigh unto hell.

Lord, I have called daily upon thee; I have stretched out my hands unto thee.

Dost thou shew wonders among the dead? or shall the dead rise up again, and praise thee?

Shall thy loving-kindness be shewed in the grave? or thy faithfulness in destruction?

Shall thy wonderful works be known in the dark? and thy righteousness in the land where all things are forgotten?

Unto thee do I cry, O Lord; and early shall my prayer come before thee.

Lord, why abhorrest thou my soul? why hidest thou thy face from me?

I am in misery, and like unto him that is at the point to die: even from my youth up thy terrors have I suffered with a troubled mind.

Thy wrathful displeasure goeth over me; and the fear of thee hath undone me.

Psalm cxli. *Verses* 1, 2.

Lord, I will call upon thee; haste thee unto me, and consider my voice when I cry unto thee.

Let my prayer be set forth in thy sight as the incense: let the lifting up of my hands be as an evening sacrifice.

Psalm lxxix. *Verses* 5; 8, 9.

Lord, how long wilt thou be angry? shall thy jealousy burn like fire for ever?

O, remember not mine old sins, but have mercy upon me; for I am come to great misery.

Help me, O God of my salvation, for the glory of thy name: O, deliver me, and be merciful to my sins, for thy name's sake.

Psalm cxliii. *Verses* 6, 7.

Lord, I stretch forth my hands unto thee; my soul gaspeth unto thee, as a thirsty land.

Hear me, O Lord, and that soon, for my spirit waxeth faint: hide not thy face from me, lest I be like unto them that go down into silence.

Psalm xiii. *Verses* 1 *to* 3.

How long wilt thou forget me, O Lord? for ever? how long wilt thou hide thy face from me?

How long shall I seek counsel in my soul, and be so vexed in my heart? how long shall mine enemies trumph over me?

Consider and hear me, O Lord my God; lighten mine eyes, that I sleep not in death.

Psalm xxx. *Verses* 6 *to* 11.

In my prosperity I said, I shall never be removed: thou, Lord, of thy goodness hadst made my state so strong.

Thou didst turn away thy face from me, and I was sore troubled.

Then cried I unto thee, O Lord; and gat me to my Lord right humbly.

What profit is there in my blood, when I go down to the pit?

Shall the dust give thanks unto thee? or shall it declare thy truth?

Hear, O Lord, and have mercy upon me; Lord, be thou my helper.

Psalm lxxvii. *Verses* 1 *to* 10.

I will cry unto God with my voice, even unto God will I cry with my voice, and he shall hearken unto me.

In the time of my trouble I sought the Lord; my sore ran and ceased not in the night season; my soul refused comfort.

When I am in heaviness I will think upon God: when my heart is vexed, I will complain.

Thou holdest mine eyes waking; I am so feeble that I can scarce speak.

I have considered the days of old, and the years that are past.

I call to remembrance my song; and in the night I commune with mine own heart, and search out my spirits.

Will the Lord absent himself for ever? and will he be no more entreated?

Is his mercy clean gone for ever? and is his promise come utterly to an end for evermore?

Hath God forgotten to be gracious? and will he shut up his loving-kindness in displeasure?

And I said, It is mine own infirmity: but I will remember the years of the right hand of the most Highest.

2 Chron xx. *Verse* 12.

O God, there is no might in us, neither know we what to do; but we lift up our eyes unto thee.

Psalm xxxv. *Verses* 17; 22.

Lord, how long wilt thou look upon this?

This thou hast seen, O Lord: hold not thy tongue, then; go not far from me, O Lord.

Psalm lxix. *Verse* 1.

Save me, O God; for the waters are come in, even unto my soul.

Psalm lxviii. *Verse* 1.

Let God arise, and let his enemies be scattered: let them also that hate him, flee before him.

Isaiah xxxviii. *Verse* 14.

O Lord, I am oppressed; undertake for me.

Psalm xxxviii. *Verse* 15.

Thou shalt answer for me, O Lord, my God.

Psalm cxxx. *Verses* 1, 2.

Out of the deep have I called unto thee, O Lord; Lord, hear my voice.

O let thine ears consider well the voice of my complaint.

Psalm lxxix. *Verse* 12.

O let the sorrowful sighing of the prisoners come before thee; according to the greatness of thy power, preserve thou those that are appointed to die.

A PRAYER BY THE PRIEST,

Begging Pardon for his own Unworthiness, and Acceptance of his Devotions for the Sick.

O Lord, it is a great presumption, that one sinner should dare to commend another to thy divine Majesty; especially, the greater, the less; and who would not fear to undertake it?

But thy commandment it is, by thy holy Apostle St. James, that when any one is sick, the elders should be called for, and should pray for the sick person; and their prayers thou dost promise to receive, and to save and forgive the sins of those so prayed for.—*James* v. 14, 15.

And now behold, O Lord, we that are no way meet, but unworthy, utterly unworthy, to sue for ought for ourselves, yet, when charity and compassion urge us, are enforced to become suitors to thee for others; even, O Lord, for this thy servant, now ready to depart this world.

In thee we hope, in thee we trust, to thee we entreat and pray, in all meekness of manner, and from the bottom of our hearts.

O Lord, that which thou mightest justly deny to our unworthiness, deny not, we beseech thee, to thine own gracious goodness.

O Lord, forgive us our sins, our great and grievous sins; oft, and many times committed; long, and many years most grievously continued; that so we may be meet to pray for others; and that so we may make our prayer unto thee in an acceptable time.

Graciously look upon our afflictions.

Pitifully behold the sorrows of our hearts.

Mercifully forgive the sins of thy people.

Favourably with mercy hear our prayers.

Both now and ever vouchsafe to hear us, O Christ.

Graciously hear us, O Christ; graciously hear us, O Lord Christ.—*Liturgy.*

A LITANY FOR THE SICK PERSON,
When in Danger of Death.

O GOD, the Father, of Heaven, have mercy upon thy servant, keep and defend *him.*

O God the Son, Redeemer of the world, have mercy upon *him*, save and deliver *him*.

O God the Holy Ghost, proceeding from the Father and the Son, have mercy upon *him*, strengthen and comfort *him*.

O holy, blessed, and glorious Trinity, have mercy upon *him*, have mercy upon *him*.

Remember not, Lord, *his* offences, nor the offences of *his* forefathers; but spare *him*, good Lord, spare thy servant, whom thou hast redeemed with thy precious blood, and be not angry with *him* for ever.

From { thy wrath and heavy indignation;
the guilt and burden of *his* sins;
the dreadful sentence of the last judgment,
Good Lord, deliver *him*.

From { the sting and terror of conscience;
the danger of impatience, distrust, and despair;
the extremity of sickness, anguish, or agony, that may any way withdraw *his* mind from thee;
Good Lord deliver *him*.

From { the bitter pangs of eternal death;
the gates of hell;
the powers of darkness;
the illusions and assaults of our ghostly enemy;
Good Lord, deliver *him*.

By thy manifold and great mercies;

By the manifold and great merits of JESUS CHRIST, thy Son;

By his
- agony and bloody sweat;
- strong crying and tears;
- bitter cross and passion;
- mighty resurrection;
- glorious ascension;
- effectual and most acceptable intercession and mediation;

And by the graces and comforts of the Holy Ghost;

Good Lord, deliver *him*.

For
- thy name's sake;
- the glory of thy name;
- thy loving mercy;
- thy truth's sake;
- thine own self;

In this
- time of *his* utmost extremity;
- *his* last and greatest need;

In the
- hour of death, and
- day of judgment;

Good Lord, deliver *him*.

Deliver *him*, O Lord, from all danger and distress; from all pains and punishments, both bodily and ghostly. Amen.

As thou didst deliver
Noah from the flood;
  so save and deliver *him*.
Lot from the fire of Sodom;
  so save and deliver *him*.

Isaac from present death;
> so save and deliver *him*.

Job from all his temptations;
> so save and deliver *him*.

Moses from the hand of Pharaoh;
> so save and deliver *him*.

Daniel from the lion's den;
> so save and deliver *him*.

Jonah from the belly of the whale;
> so save and deliver *him*.

And, as thou hast delivered thy blessed saints and servants from all their terrors and torments;

So save and deliver *his* soul, and receive it to thy mercy.

WE sinners do beseech thee to hear us, good Lord.
> That it may please thee to remember *him* with the favour thou bearest unto thy people, and to visit *him* with thy salvation:—*Ps.* cvi. 4.

We beseech thee to hear us, good Lord.
> That it may please thee to save and deliver *his* soul from the power of the enemy, lest, as a lion, he devour it, and tear it in pieces, if there be none to help:—*Psalm* vii. 1, 2.

We beseech thee to hear us, good Lord.
> That it may please thee to be merciful, and to forgive all *his* sins and misdeeds, which by the malice of the devil, or by *his* own frailty, *he* hath at any time of *his* life committed against thee:

We beseech thee to hear us, good Lord.

That it may please thee not to lay to *his* charge, what in the lust of the eye, the pride, the vanity, or superfluity of life, *he* hath committed against thee :—1 *John* ii. 16.

We beseech thee to hear us, good Lord.

That it may please thee not to lay to *his* charge, what in the fierceness of *his* wrath, or in the eagerness of an angry spirit, *he* hath committed against thee :

We beseech thee to hear us, good Lord.

That it may please thee not to lay to *his* charge, what in vain and idle words, in the looseness and slipperiness of the tongue, *he* hath committed against thee ;

We beseech thee to hear us, good Lord.

That it may please thee to make *him* partaker of all thy mercies and promises in CHRIST JESUS :

We beseech thee to hear us, good Lord.

That it may please thee to vouchsafe unto *his* soul the estate of joy, happiness, and immortality, with all thy blessed saints, in thy heavenly kingdom :

We beseech thee to hear us, good Lord.

That it may please thee to grant unto *his* body rest and peace, and a part in the blessed resurrection unto life and glory :

We beseech thee to hear us, good Lord.

SON of God, we beseech thee to hear us.

O Lord God, Lamb of God, that takest away the sins of the world,

Have mercy upon thy servant.

Thou that takest away the sins of the world,
Have mercy upon *him*.

Thou that takest away the sins of the world,
Grant *him* thy peace.

Thou that sittest on the right hand of God the Father,
Have mercy upon *him*.

Lord, have mercy upon *him*.

Christ, have mercy upon *him*.

Lord, have mercy upon *him*.

Our Father, which art in heaven, &c.

O Lord, deal not with *him* after *his* sins;
Neither reward *him* according to *his* iniquities.

O God, merciful Father, that despisest not the sighing of a contrite heart, nor the desire of such as be sorrowful, mercifully assist our prayers, that we make before thee in all our troubles and adversities, whensoever they oppress us; at such times, especially, when our greatest and most grievous extremities are ready to oppress us. And graciously hear us, O Lord, that those evils, those illusions, terrors, and assaults, which thine or our enemy worketh against us, be brought to nought, and by the providence of thy goodness they may be dispersed; that we, thy servants, being swallowed up by no temptations, may evermore give thanks unto thee in thy Holy Church, through Jesus Christ our Lord. Amen.

AN HUMBLE RECOGNITION OF HUMAN FRAILTY,

And a Deprecation against Falling from God.

(From the Burial Service.)

In the midst of life we are in death: of whom, then, may we seek for succour, but of thee, O Lord, who for our sins art most justly displeased with us?

Yet, O Lord most holy, O God most mighty, O holy and most merciful Father, deliver us not over to the bitter pains of eternal death.

Thou knowest, Lord, the secrets of our hearts; shut not the ears of thy mercy to our prayer: but spare us, Lord most holy, O God most mighty, O immortal and most merciful Father, thou most worthy Judge eternal, suffer us not in our last hour for any pains of death to fall from thee.

AN AFFECTIONATE RECOMMENDATION OF THE SICK TO GOD'S MERCY;

Grounded upon his Special Relations to God, and the Sincerity of his Soul.

I. O Lord,

We commend unto thee the soul of this thy servant.

He is

The work of thy hands;

Despise not, O Lord, the work of thine own hands.—*Psalm* xxxviii. 8.

The likeness of thy image;

Suffer not, O Lord, thy image to be utterly defaced.—*Gen.* i. 27.

The price of thy blood;

Let not so great a price be cast away.—1 *Cor.* vi. 20.

A Christian;

The name of thy Son is called upon him;—*Jer.* xiv. 9.

For thy name's sake be good unto thy name.—*Psalm* lxxix. 9.

He is thine; O, save *him*.—*Psalm* cxix. 94.

Give not over what is thine, unto the will of the enemy.—*Psalm* xli. 2.

Though *he* hath sinned, yet thy name hath *he* not denied; but called upon it, and confessed it unto *his* life's end: and there is no other name under heaven, but thine, whereby *he* hopeth to be saved.—*Acts* iv. 12.

Though *he* hath sinned, yet hath *he* not covered *his* sin, (*Job* xxxi. 33.) nor excused it, (2 *Cor.* xii. 19.) but hath confessed it, and been sorry for it, and wisheth even for tears of blood, wherewith to lament it.

Though *he* hath sinned, yet others also have sinned against *him*, whom *he* from *his* heart forgiveth, and desireth forgiveness of them at thy gracious hands.—*Matt.* vi. 14.

O, stablish thy word unto thy servant, (*Psalm* cxix. 38.) and let *him* not be disappointed of his hope.—*Verse* 116.

Though *he* hath sinned, yet in thee *he* trusteth; O, suffer *him* not to be utterly confounded for ever.—1 *Pet.* ii. 6.

Though *he* hath sinned, yet *he* seeketh thee: and thou, Lord, never failest them that seek thee.—*Psalm* ix. 10.

Though *he* hath sinned, yet *he* cometh to thee: and of them that come to thee, thou castest none out.—*John* vi. 37.

II. O Lord,

Let not the guiltiness of a sinner more prevail to condemn, than the gracious goodness of a most merciful Father to acquit and pardon.

O, let not the unrighteousness of man make the goodness of God without effect.—*Rom.* iii. 3.

O Lord, do not so remember the ingratitude of this thy child, as thereby to forget the compassion and kindness of a Father.

Do not so think upon our sins, as thereby to forget thine own nature and property, which is always to have mercy.—*Liturgy.*

Do not so remember our sins, as thereby to forget thine own name, which is JESUS, a most kind and loving Saviour.

III. O Lord,

If in our life thy life hath not sufficiently appeared, yet let not thy death in our death also lose its full power and effect.

Suffer not, O Lord, in both, so great a price to perish.

Lose not, O Lord, that which thou hast saved; since thou camest to save that which was lost.—*Matt.* xviii. 11.

That which was so dear for thee to save, suffer not to be lost as a thing of no value.

A PRAYER FOR MERCY AND DIVINE ASSISTANCE,
To uphold the Sick Person in his Affliction.

HAVE mercy upon thy servant, O Lord; consider the pains which *he* suffereth; thou, who only dost deliver from the gates of death.—*Psalm* ix. 13.

Shew *him* thy marvellous loving-kindness, thou that art the Saviour of them which put their trust in thee.—*Psalm* xvii. 7.

O, keep *him* as the apple of thine eye: hide *him* under the shadow of thy wings.—*Verse* 8.

O let thy merciful loving-kindness be *his* comfort, according to thy word unto thy servant.—*Psalm* cxix. 76.

He is troubled above measure; be merciful to *him*, O Lord, according to thy goodness.—*Verse* 107.

O consider *his* adversity, and deliver *him*; for *he* is brought very low.—*Psalm* cxlii. 7.

His eyes long sore for thy word, saying, O when wilt thou comfort me?—*Psalm* cxix. 82.

His eyes are wasted away with looking for thy

health, and for the word of thy righteousness.—*Verse* 123.

O think upon *him*, as concerning thy word; wherein thou hast caused *him* to put *his* trust.—*Verse* 49.

O look upon *him*, and be merciful unto *him*, as thou usest to do unto those that love thy name.—*Verse* 132.

Cast *him* not away in the time of *his* weakness; forsake *him* not now, when *his* strength faileth *him*.—*Psalm* lxxi. 8.

In the multitude of the sorrows that *he* hath in *his* heart, let thy comforts refresh *his* soul.—*Psalm* xciv. 19.

O Lord, when *he* is oppressed, comfort thou *him*.—*Isaiah* xxxviii. 14.

O Lord, let thy strength be made perfect in *his* weakness.—2 *Cor.* xii. 9.

Let no temptation oppress *him*, but such as is common to thy children: but, as thou art faithful, O God, suffer *him* not to be tempted, above what *he* is able: but, with the temptation, good Lord, give a happy issue, that *he* may be able to overcome it.—1 *Cor.* x. 13.

O Lord, though *he* be afflicted on every side, yet let *him* not be distressed; though in want of some of thy comforts, yet not of all; though chastened, yet not forsaken; though cast down, yet not destroyed.—2 *Cor.* iv. 8, 9.

A PRAYER FOR THE GRACE OF GOD, AND PARDON FOR THE SINS OF THE SICK.

REMEMBER thy servant, O Lord, according to the favour that thou bearest unto thy children; O, visit *him* with thy salvation;

That *he* may see the felicity of thy chosen, and rejoice in the gladness of thy saints, and give thanks with thine inheritance.—*Psalm* cvi. 4, 5.

O, remember not *his* former sins, but have mercy upon *him*, O Lord, and that soon; for *he* is come to great extremity:

Help *him*, O Lord God of *his* salvation, for the glory of thy name; O, deliver him, and be merciful unto *his* sins for thy name's sake.—*Psalm* lxxix. 8, 9.

Call to remembrance, O Lord, thy tender mercies, and thy loving-kindnesses which have been ever of old;

O, remember not the sins and offences of *his* youth; but according to thy mercy think thou upon *him*, O Lord, for thy goodness.—*Psalm* xxv. 5, 6.

Cleanse *him*, O Lord, from *his* secret faults;— *Psalm* xix. 12.

From whatsoever *he* hath done amiss,

By { thought, word, or deed; ignorance or error, frailty or negligence;

In excess, or in defect;

By { leaving good undone, or doing evil;

In public or private;
By day or night;
Against { *his* { thee; neighbour; own body; }
Before or since *his* effectual calling;
By *him*self or by others;
Remembered or forgotten;

Cleanse *him* from them all, O Lord, even from them all;—*Psalm* li. 2.

Lay none of them to *his* charge;—*Acts* vii. 60.

Cast them all behind thee;—*Isaiah* xxxviii. 17.

Bury them; drown them;—*Micah* vii. 19.

Scatter them as the mist, and as the morning cloud;—*Isaiah* xliv. 22.

Make them to vanish away, and come to nothing.—*Job* vii. 9.

And whereinsoever *his* conscience most accuseth *him*, therein, O Lord, be thou most merciful.

O, enter not into judgment with thy servant; for in thy sight shall no man living be justified.—*Psalm* cxliii. 2.

If thou, Lord, wilt be extreme to mark what is done amiss; O Lord, who may abide it?—*Psalm* cxxx. 3.

But, good Lord, one deep calleth another (*Ps.* xlii. 9.); the deep of our misery the deep of thy mercy.

Wherein sin hath abounded, there let grace more abound:—*Rom.* v. 20.

And in and through all sins and offences, O Lord, let thy mercy rejoice against thy justice.—*James* ii. 13.

O Lord, hear; O Lord, forgive; O Lord, hearken and do.—*Dan.* ix. 19.

Delay not, O Lord; for *his* spirit fainteth: hide not thy face from *him*, lest *he* be like unto them that go down into the pit.—*Psalm* cxliii. 7.

Be favourable, O Lord, be favourable;

For thy $\begin{Bmatrix} \text{name} \\ \text{truth} \\ \text{mercy} \end{Bmatrix}$'s sake;

For thy $\begin{Bmatrix} \text{many} \\ \text{great} \\ \text{wonderful} \end{Bmatrix}$ $\begin{matrix} \text{mercies'} \\ \text{sake;} \end{matrix}$

For thine own self, O Lord,

Our $\begin{Bmatrix} \text{Creator and Redeemer;} \\ \begin{Bmatrix} \text{Lord} \\ \text{King} \end{Bmatrix} \text{ and our } \begin{Bmatrix} \text{Father;} \\ \text{God.} \end{Bmatrix} \end{Bmatrix}$

A COMMENDATION OF THE SOUL TO GOD.

LORD, now lettest thou thy servant depart in peace.—*Luke* ii. 29.

Into thy hands, O God, we commend *his* spirit; for thou hast redeemed it, O Lord, thou God of truth.—*Psalm* xxxi. 6.

Bring *his* soul out of prison, that it may praise thee.—*Psalm* cxlii. 9.

O, deliver *him* from the body of this death.—*Rom.* vii. 24.

Say unto *his* soul, I am thy salvation.—*Psalm* xxxv. 3.

Say unto *him*, To-day shalt thou be with me in Paradise.—*Luke* xxiii. 43.

Let *him* now feel the salvation of Jesus; let *him* now feel the anointing of Christ; (1 *John* ii. 27.) even the oil of gladness wherewith thou art anointed. —*Psalm* xlv. 8. *Heb.* i. 9.

Guide thou *him* through the valley of the shadow of death.—*Psalm* xxiii. 4.

Let *him* see the goodness of the Lord in the land of the living.—*Psalm* xxvii. 15.

O Lord, command *his* spirit to be received up to thee in peace.—*Acts* vii. 59.

O Lord, bid *him* come unto thee.—*Matt.* xiv. 28.

Lord Jesus, receive *his* spirit (*Acts* vii. 59.); and open to *him* the gates of everlasting glory.—*Psalm* xxiv. 7.

Let thy loving Spirit lead *him* forth into the land of righteousness (*Psalm* cxliii. 10.); into thy holy hill (*Psalm* xv. 1.); into thy heavenly kingdom.— 2 *Tim.* iv. 18.

Send thine angel to meet *him*, and to carry *him* into Abraham's bosom.—*Luke* xvi. 22.

Place *him* in the habitation of light and peace, of joy and gladness.

Receive *him* into the arms of thy mercy; and give *him* an inheritance with thy saints in light: —*Col.* i. 12.

There to reign with thy elect angels, thy blessed saints departed, thy holy prophets, and glorious apostles, in all joy, glory, felicity, and blessedness, for ever and ever. Amen.

COMFORTABLE SCRIPTURES TO FRIENDS OF THE DECEASED.

Precious in the sight of the Lord is the death of his saints.—*Psalm* cxvi. 13.

I heard a voice from heaven, saying unto me, Write, Blessed are the dead, which die in the Lord; for they rest from their labours; and their works do follow them.—*Rev.* xiv. 13.

A GENERAL CONFESSION OF SINS,

Collected out of the Holy Prophets and Apostles.

Moses.

We have sinned, O Lord.—*Exod.* xxxii. 30.

Thou hast set our misdeeds before thee, and our secret sins in the light of thy countenance.—*Psalm* xc. 8.

Return, O Lord, how long? and be gracious unto thy servants.—*Verse* 13.

Job.

I have sinned: what shall I do unto thee, O thou Preserver of men? Why hast thou set me as a mark against thee, so that I am a burthen to myself?—*Job* vii. 20.

That I am wicked, woe is me.—*Job* x. 15.

Be favourable unto me, O Lord, and render unto

me my righteousness: say concerning me, O Lord, Deliver him, for I have found a ransom.—*Job* xxxiii. 26; 24.

Yet, if thou slay me, will I trust in thee.—*Job* xiii. 15.

David.

My misdeeds have prevailed against me; O, be thou merciful unto my sins.—*Psalm* lxv. 3.

I have gone astray like a sheep that is lost; O, seek thy servant, for I do not forget thy commandments.—*Psalm* cxix. 176.

We have sinned with our fathers, we have done amiss, and dealt wickedly.—*Psalm* cvi. 6.

For thy name's sake, O Lord, be merciful unto our sin; for it is great.—*Psalm* xxv. 10.

My foot hath slipped; let thy mercy, O Lord, hold me up.—*Psalm* xciv. 18.

Isaiah.

Behold, thou art wroth; for we have sinned:

We have been as an unclean thing; and all our righteousness as filthy rags:

We all do fade as a leaf; and our iniquities, like the wind, have taken us away.

But now, O Lord, thou art our Father; we are the clay, and thou art the Potter; we all are the work of thy hand.

Be not wroth very sore, O Lord, neither remember our iniquity for ever: see, we beseech thee; remember, we are all thy people.—*Isaiah* lxiv. 5, 6; 8, 9.

Jeremiah.

O Lord, our iniquities testify against us; our backslidings are many; we have sinned against thee.

Yet deal with us according to thy name: for thou, O Lord, art in the midst of us, and we are called by thy name; O, leave us not.

O Lord, the Hope of Israel, the Saviour thereof in time of trouble, forsake us not.—*Jer.* xiv. 7; 9; 8.

Daniel.

We have sinned, O Lord, we have committed iniquity, we have done wickedly: yea, we have rebelled, even by departing from thy precepts, and from thy judgments.

O Lord, righteousness belongeth unto thee, but unto us confusion and shame of face, because of all the trespasses that we have trespassed against thee.

Yet mercies and forgivenesses belong to thee, O Lord our God, though we have rebelled against thee.

O Lord, according to all thy righteousness, I beseech thee, let thine anger and thy fury be turned away from me; and cause thy face to shine upon thy servant.

O my God, incline thine ear and hear; open thine eyes, and behold my desolations: for we do not present our supplications before thee for our righteousnesses, but for thy manifold and great mercies.

O Lord, hear: O Lord, forgive: O Lord, hearken and do: defer not, for thine own sake, O my God.—*Dan.* ix. 5; 7; 9; 16, 17, 18, 19.

Jonah.

O Lord, in observing vanities I have forsaken mine own mercy.

For which I am cast out of the sight of thine eyes. Yet I remember thee, O Lord; and will look yet again toward thy holy temple.

O Lord, hear and have mercy.—*Jonah* ii. 8, 4; 2.

The Prodigal Child.

Father, I have sinned against heaven and before thee, and am no more worthy to be called thy son:

But forgive me, and make as one of the meanest of thy hired servants.—*Luke* xv. 18, 19.

God, be merciful to me a sinner.—*Luke* xviii. 13.

Jesus, Master, have mercy on us.—*Luke* xvii. 13.

Have mercy on me, O Lord, thou Son of David.—*Matt.* xv. 22.

Lord, help me.—*Verse* 25.

Even the dogs, Lord, eat of the crumbs which fall from thy table.—*Verse* 27.

St. Paul.

O Lord, I am carnal, and sold under sin:

And in me (that is, in my flesh) dwelleth no good thing.—*Rom.* vii. 14; 18.

The good things which I would, I do not: the evil which I would not, that I do.—*Verse* 15.

Though I delight in the law, according to the inner man,

Yet I feel another law in my nature, warring against the law of my mind, and bringing me into captivity to the law of sin.—*Verses* 22, 23.

O wretched man that I am! Who shall deliver me from the body of this death?—*Verse* 24.

But this is a faithful saying, and worthy of all acceptation, that Christ Jesus came into the world to save sinners; of whom l am chief.—1 *Tim.* i. 15.

St. Peter.

We have spent the time past of our life, after the lusts of the Gentiles, walking in lasciviousness, lusts, revellings, banquettings, and other excesses.—1 *Pet.* iv. 3.

But thou hast redeemed us, O Lord, by the precious blood of Christ, the undefiled Lamb.—1 *Pet.* i. 18, 19.

Have mercy upon us in that name, beside which thou hast given none other under heaven, whereby we must be saved.—*Acts* iv. 12.

St. John.

If we say that we have no sin, we deceive ourselves, and the truth is not in us.—1 *John* i. 8.

If our heart condemn us, God is greater than our heart, and knoweth all things.—1 *John* iii. 20.

But we confess our sins, and, confessing them, we have an Advocate with the Father, Jesus Christ the righteous, and he is the propitiation for our sins.—1 *John* ii. 1, 2.

St. James.

In many things we offend all.—*James* iii. 2.

But, Lord, let thy mercy rejoice against thy justice.—*James* ii. 13.

A CONFESSION OF SINS,

According to the Divisions of the Decalogue.

I.

Touching thee, O Lord, I have been full of roving imaginations, and evil thoughts.

I have not studied to seek and know thee as I ought to do.

Knowing thee, I have not glorified thee, nor given thanks to thee accordingly.—*Rom.* i. 21.

I have doubted thy promises, and distrusted thy help.

I have made flesh mine arm (*Jer.* xvii. 5.), and hoped for prosperity from man, rather than from thee.

I have not performed the duty of invocation with that reverence I owe to thee.

I have not been thankful; and especially not for thy chastisements.

II.

I have not worshipped thee in spirit and in truth. —*John* iv. 24.

I have drawn near to thee with my lips, but my heart hath been far from thee.—*Mark* vii. 6.

I have been more careful of the outward and ceremonial, than of the inward and spiritual, part of thy worship.

III.

I have, without due regard, taken thy name into my mouth.

I have, with rash oaths and eager execrations, oftentimes abused it.

I have not given occasion to others to sanctify thy name; but have caused it to be evil spoken of through mine own evil dealing.—2 *Pet.* ii. 2.

I have not duly regarded and reverenced those things, whereon thy name is imprinted.

IV.

I have not brought that care which I should have brought to thy sabbath and thy sanctuary.

I have not hesitated to absent myself from thy holy assemblies, without sufficient cause.—*Heb.* x. 25.

I have not spent the days assigned to holy exercises, chiefly upon them; but have followed too much mine own private business in them.

I have been content in them with the use of the means alone, without any practice at all.

V.

I have not so reverently spoken, nor so dutifully carried myself, toward some whom thou hast placed over me, as was meet I should do.

I have not so carefully prayed for them, as was required of me.

I have not opposed such as used irreverent terms toward them:

Especially toward those, who have had the government of my soul in charge.

VI.

I have not wished or provided for the good of my neighbour as I should have done; but rather been angry, quarrelsome, and ill-disposed toward him; and sought revenge upon every light injury.

I have not had that compassion on the poor that I should have had; nor ministered to their necessities:

I have not defended them, as I might, against the wrongs of others.

I have not rejoiced in the good success of my neighbour; but envied his welfare.

VII.

I have not possessed my vessel in sanctification and honour (1 *Thess.* iv. 4.); nor preserved it

from pollution, as the temple of God should be.—
1 *Cor.* iii. 16, 17.

I have suffered my fancy to wander licentiously.

Mine ears and tongue I have not kept, as I should do.

I have not eschewed the occasions of lust, nor made a covenant with mine eyes.—*Job* xxxi. 1.

I have not kept under my body, nor brought it into subjection with abstinence.—1 *Cor.* ix. 27.

I have more studiously, and with more cost, administered to my flesh than to my spirit.

VIII.

I have not reckoned godliness to be gain (1 *Tim.* vi. 6.); nor been content with my estate (*Phil.* iv. 11.); but have wished for higher.

I have not been so exact in paying and in dealing with those I have dealt withal, as in justice I was bound to be.

I have by undue means interverted, to mine own use, that which was not mine.

I have not been willing, out of that, whereof I had more than enough, to bestow on the relief of the needy.

IX.

I have not been so studious of speaking the truth, as I should have been.

I have been desirous to seem, and to be reputed, more than I was.

I have not had that care for the good name of my brother, that I was bound to have.

I have not so hated flattery, as I should have done.

I have not so upheld and defended the truth, as was meet I should do.

X.

I have been full of wandering desires, wicked affections, unlawful concupiscences, evil suspicions and surmises, and inordinate lusts, touching my neighbour, and that which is his.

THE TRIUMPH OF MERCY;

In many Gradual Expressions and Remembrances, propounded in Holy Scripture.

GOD, in his mercy, is
Gentle and forgiving;—2 *Cor.* x. 1. *Gen.* xviii. 32.
> Takes all in the better part; if it will admit any good sense, so construes it.

Meek;—2 *Cor.* x. 1.
> Not irritable; not easily stirred up or provoked.

Willing to shut his eyes;—*Wisd.* xi. 24.
> Sees, and sees not: makes as though he did not see.

Prone to wink;—*Acts* xvii. 30.

Overlooks our sins, looks not at them.

Prone to pass by;—*Micah* vii. 18.

Passeth over our sins, when we repent.

Forbearing;—*Rom.* ii. 4.

When he cannot but see, yet is he patient.

Long-suffering;—*Rom.* ii. 4. *Neh.* ix. 21; 30.

Forbears long, many times, many years.

Asking how;—*Hosea* vi. 4. *and* xi. 8.

When he can suffer no longer, yet stands, as over Ephraim, asking, *How shall I?* and yet endures.

Waiting to be gracious;—*Isaiah* xxx. 18.

And when he can forbear no longer, but punish he must, he doth it not willingly, (*Lament.* iii. 33.) but against his inclination.

And when he punisheth, he doth it without suffering his whole displeasure to arise, (*Psalm* lxxviii. 39.) but containing himself and his anger.

He doth it not according to our deserts, (*Psalm* ciii. 10.) no, not near so much.

Not long; it endureth but the twinkling of an eye.—*Psalm* xxx. 5. *and* ciii. 9. *Isaiah* liv. 7, 8.

He thinketh every stripe double (*Isaiah* xl. 2.); is quickly weary.

In his wrath remembereth mercy.—*Hab.* iii. 2.

Repenteth him of the evil.—*Joel* ii. 13.

Is moved with the sight of our miseries.—*Ps.* cvi. 43, 44.

Is soon and easily appeased.—*Isaiah* xxx. 19. *and* lv. 7. *Matt.* xi. 30.

Hath mercy;

Hath multitudes of mercy ;

Hath compassion ;

The bowels of { compassion ;—1 *John* iii. 17.
a parent ;—*Psalm* ciii. 13.
a mother ;—*Isaiah* xlix. 15.

Many bowels.—*James* v. 11.

Forgives, pardons.—*Matt.* xviii. 27.

Is reconciled.—2 *Cor.* v. 18.

Takes into favour again.—*Luke* xv. 22, 23.

Receives to grace.—*Rom.* iii. 24.

For all have sinned, and come short of the glory of God.—*Verse* 23.

In his angels he hath found folly; and the stars are not clean in his sight.—*Job* iv. 18. *and* xv. 15. *and* xxv. 5.

But he hath not made all men for nought.—*Psalm* lxxxix. 46.

Yet if God should be extreme to mark what is done amiss, who were able to abide it?—*Psalm* cxxx. 3.

If he should enter into judgment with his servants, no man living should be justified in his sight.—*Psalm* cxliii. 2.

None were able to answer him one for a thousand: no, not Job himself.—*Job* ix. 3.

Therefore God hath concluded all under sin, that he might have mercy upon all.—*Rom.* xi. 32.

He would have all men to be saved.—1 *Tim.* ii. 4.

He is not willing that any should perish; but that all should come to repentance.—2 *Pet.* iii. 9.

He hath no pleasure in the death of the wicked; but that he turn from his way, and live.—*Ezek.* xxxiii. 11.

LET all that know their sin,—*Psalm* li. 3.

Know it, and acknowledge it;—*Psalm* xxxii. 5. *Luke* xv. 18.

Acknowledge it, and be sorry for it;—*Psalm* xxxviii. 18.

Be sorry for it, and be ready to forsake it;—*Prov.* xxviii. 13.

And not only to forsake it, but to judge themselves for it;—1 *Cor.* xi. 31. *Ezek.* xxxvi. 31. 1 *Cor.* ix. 27.

And to punish themselves for it:—2 *Cor.* vii. 11.

By the fruits of mortification;—*Joel* ii. 12, 13. *Jonah* iii. 5.

Accompanied with

Prayer;—*Psalm* xxxii. 7. *Acts* viii. 22.

And alms;—*Isaiah* lviii. 7. *Prov.* xvi. 6. *Dan.* iv. 27.

At the estimation of the priest;—*Levit.* vi. 6.

Who may forgive us in the person of Christ;—*John* viii. 11. *and* xx. 23. 2 *Cor.* ii. 10.

And which his mercy is not only for common and ordinary sinners, but for the chief; such as were Manasses, Paul, David, Peter, Rahab, Mary Magdalene, Jonah, the thief on the cross;

Such as were the Corinthians;—1 *Cor.* v. 1. *and* vi. 11.

Such as were the Jews, his betrayers and his murderers.—*Acts* iii. 13, 14, 15.

David was a man after God's own heart;—1 *Sam.* xiii. 14. *Acts* xiii. 22.

Christ is the Son of David;—*Matt.* xxii. 42.

And David forgave Shimei,—2 *Sam.* xix. 23.

And wept for his rebellious son Absalom.—2 *Sam.* xviii. 33.

The Preface, or Style, of the Law.

THE Lord, the Lord God,
Merciful and gracious,
Long-suffering, and abundant in goodness and truth, keeping mercy for thousands, and forgiving.—*Exod.* xxxiv. 6, 7.

The Discourse of Elihu.—Job xxxiii. 23, 24.

IF there be a messenger with him, an interpreter, one among a thousand, to shew unto man his uprightness;

Then he is gracious unto him, and saith, Deliver him from going down to the pit; I have found a ransom.

O, TASTE and see, how gracious the Lord is.—*Psalm* xxxiv. 8. 1 *Peter* ii. 3.

His mercy is sweet.—*Psalm* cix. 20.

His mercies are many.—*Psalm* cvi. 44.

There is a multitude of them.—*Psalm* lxix. 17. *and* v. 7. *and* li. 1.

There is a plenteous redemption.—*Psalm* cxxx. 7.

His mercies are great;—*Psalm* lxxxvi. 5. *and* cxix. 156.

Great in
- magnitude;—*Isaiah* liv. 7.
- height;—*Psalm* ciii. 11. *and* cviii. 4. *and* xxxvi. 5.
- depth;—*Psalm* xlii. 9.
- length.—*Psalm* xxvi. 3. & *Psalm* cxxxvi.

There is no end of his salvation.—*Ps.* lxxi. 13.

Mercy shall be set up for ever.—*Ps.* lxxxix. 2.

His mercy is over all his works.—*Ps.* cxlv. 9.

As is his majesty, so is his mercy.—*Ecclus.* ii. 18.

His property is always to have mercy,—*Rom.* xi. 32.

He is the Father of mercies,—2 *Cor.* i. 3.

He is mercy itself.—*Psalm* lix. 17.

He was so merciful, that he forgave their misdeeds, and destroyed them not;

Yea, many a time turned he his wrath away, and would not suffer his whole displeasure to arise;

For he considered they were but dust.—*Psalm* lxxviii. 38, 39; 40.

The Lord waiteth that he may have mercy upon you.—*Isaiah* xxx. 18.

In the father of the lost child, behold his image. —*Luke* xv. 22.

Without shedding of blood is no remission of sins. —*Heb.* ix. 22.

God hath concluded all under sin, that he might have mercy upon all.—*Rom.* xi. 32.

Where sin aboundeth, there grace doth more abound.—*Rom.* v. 20.

Mercy rejoiceth against judgment.—*James* ii. 13.

In this hath God commended his love toward us, in that, while we were yet sinners, Christ died for us.—*Rom.* v. 8.

This is a faithful saying, and worthy of all acceptation, that Christ Jesus came into the world to save sinners.—1 *Tim.* i. 15.

Christ suffered once for our sins, the just for the unjust, that he might offer us to God.—1 *Pet.* iii. 18.

We have an Advocate with the Father, Jesus Christ the righteous;

And he is the propitiation for our sins; and not for ours only, but also for the sins of the whole world.—1 *John* ii. 1, 2.

I came not to call the righteous, but sinners to repentance.—*Matt.* ix. 13.

Come unto me, all ye that labour and are heavy-laden, and I will refresh you.—*Matt.* xi. 28.

Of them that come to me, I will cast none out. —*John* vi. 37.

Lord, thou never failest them that seek thee — *Psalm* ix. 10.

SPIRITUAL COMFORT AND CONFIDENCE,

Issuing from the Contemplation of God's Goodness.

Why art thou so full of heaviness, O my soul? and why art thou so disquieted within me?

O, put thy trust in God; for I shall yet give him thanks: for he is the help of my countenance, and my God.—*Psalm* xlii. 6, 7; 14, 15. *and* xliii. 5, 6.

Return then unto thy rest, O my soul; for the Lord hath been gracious to thee.—*Psalm* cxvi. 7.

If the Lord had not helped me, it had not failed but my soul had been put to silence:

In the midst of the troubles that I had in my heart, thy comforts have refreshed my soul.—*Psalm* xciv. 17; 19.

Nevertheless, though I am sometimes afraid, yet put I my trust in the Lord.—*Psalm* lvi. 3.

Nevertheless, my soul, wait thou still upon God, for of him cometh my salvation:

He verily is my hope, and my strength; he is my defence, so that I shall not greatly fall.—*Psalm* lxii. 5, 6.

Let us go with boldness unto the throne of grace, that we may find mercy in time of need.—*Heb.* iv. 16.

DEVOUT EJACULATIONS,

Grounded on the Consideration of Human Frailty, and of Divine Providence and Mercy.

O LORD of life and death, of sickness and health, and of all things thereunto belonging;

By whose appointment we are born; and, again, by whose appointment we die:

Our time is in thy hand; (*Psalm* xxxi. 17.) and unto thee belong the issues of death.—*Psalm* lxviii. 20.

Thou that hatest nothing that thou hast made, nor dost ever utterly forsake the work of thine own hands;—*Psalm* cxxxviii. 8.

Thou that art a defence for the oppressed; a refuge in the needful time of trouble;—*Psalm* ix. 9.

Thou that never failest them that seek thee;—*Verse* 10.

And to whom none ever prayeth without hope to be heard;

Thou, that hast promised, that the poor shall not alway be forgotten; that the patient abiding of the meek shall not perish for ever:—*Psalm* ix. 18.

For the comfortless troubles' sake of the needy, and for the deep sighing of the poor,—*Psalm* xii. 5.

Arise, O Lord, and men shall know that it is thy hand, and that it is thou, Lord, that hast done it.—*Psalm* cix. 25, 26.

O LORD, whose mercy reacheth unto the heavens, and whose faithfulness unto the clouds;—*Psalm* xxxvi. 5. *and* lvii. 11.

Of whose mercies there is neither number nor end;

The greatness of whose goodness is not shut up under any time;

Who callest into thy vineyard even at the eleventh hour;—*Matt.* xx. 6, 7.

Who rulest not with rigour, but governest with meekness the things thou hast made:

Thou that killest and makest alive; that bringest down to the grave, and bringest up again;—1 *Sam.* ii. 6.

Thou that hatest nothing which thou hast made; —*Wisd.* xi. 24.

That hast concluded all under sin; that thou mightest have mercy upon all:—*Rom.* xi. 32.

O Lord, the Saviour and the saving health of all thy faithful;

The Fountain of grace and goodness;

The Father of mercies, and God of all comfort; —2 *Cor.* i. 3.

Thou that upholdest all such as fall, and liftest up all those that are down;—*Psalm* cxlv. 14.

Thou that healest the broken in heart, and givest medicine to heal their sickness;—*Psalm* cxlvii. 3.

The consolation of them that be in heaviness;

The strength of them that be in weakness;

The health of them that be in sickness:
  Hear, O Lord, and have mercy;
  Look down from Heaven;
  Behold and visit;
  Visit with thy salvation.—*Psalm* lxxx. 14.

APPENDIX.

From the Volume of English MS., mentioned in the Preface.

1. A PRAYER FOR THE KING.

KINGS are Gods upon earth; yet, O Lord, they are but thy servants.

They rule kingdoms; yet the chariot of their empire turneth over and over, unless thou teach their hands how to hold the reins.

More than men they are amongst men; yet less than themselves, if they break thy laws.

Since, then, they are thy stewards, and trusted with much, it is a great reckoning to which they must answer.

Lay therefore, O Lord, thy right hand on the head of our gracious sovereign Lord, King Charles.

Fasten his crown close to his temples, that no treason may lift it off; bind it round about with olive branches, and let peace dwell under the circle of it.

Plant a guard of angels about his bed, and a troop of saints about his throne, that his sleep may be golden slumbers, and his watchings divine meditations.

Pour, O Lord, thy graces into his bosom, that all his actions may advance thy glory.

Be thou, O Lord, his armour in the day of battle; and, like the wings of an eagle, let thy arms cover him in the sunshine of peace.

Make him, O God, a priest in thy Church, a father in the commonwealth, a shepherd over thy flock, a captain in thy quarrel, and, O my God, a conqueror in thy wars.

Crown him, O Lord, with number of years, as thou didst crown his youth with the inheritance of kingdoms.

Let the dial of his life move slowly on, and suffer not his old age to strike, till those that now stand up about him, like the tender branches of the vine, be seen growing on the banks of this same kingdom, like rows of tall cedars.

Let his reign, O Lord, be like the reign of Methusalem, his knowledge like the wisdom of Solomon, his offspring blessed like the seed of Abraham, and suffer not the face of thine anointed to be cast down.—2 *Chron.* vi. 42.

Give him, O God, David's soul, but suffer him not to fall into David's sins; teach him to number his people, not to make thee angry with him, but to make him love them, and them him, and thee, O Lord, them all.

All the strings of their hearts tie close to his bosom, that they may all move as to one centre; that their happiness may be his fortress, their prosperity his riches, the hour of his pleasure the sweetest of their contentment.

These, and what other benefits be fit for so good, so sweet a prince, grant him, O Lord, for the safety of thy church, the peace and honour of this kingdom, and the relief of thy now poor and much afflicted people; even for Jesus Christ's sake. Amen.

2. A PRAYER TO BE USED IN THESE DANGEROUS TIMES OF WAR.

O ALMIGHTY and just God, which art the Author of all goodness, look down upon the distressed estate of us thy servants, ready to be devoured with the sword, and to be utterly rooted out of the land of the living by reason of our many and manifold transgressions.

Lord, we have sinned and gone astray from thy commandments; and have delayed to repent our iniquities: wherefore in thy justice thou visitest our transgressions with the rod, and our sins with scourges.—*Psalm* lxxxix. 32.

We have put behind our backs all thy favourable and fatherly admonitions, and have slighted all the opportunities of amending our sinful and wicked lives; and therefore are these plagues deservedly come upon us.—*Gen.* xlii. 21.

Yet, O Lord, with thee there is mercy, and with thee is plenteous redemption.—*Psalm* cxxx. 7.

Thou, O Lord, art able to bring our souls from

the depths of hell, and to raise us from the brink of the bottomless pit of perdition.

And because whatsoever thou canst do for us, thou wilt do, if we wretched sinners but ask aright with faith and repentance;

Save us, O Lord, we beseech thee, from the hands of our enemies, and evermore mightily defend us.—*Liturgy*.

Especially in these miserable and calamitous times, wherein we are every moment threatened to be devoured, succour us with thy might;

And, if it be thy will to sift and try us, give us patience in our afflictions, and confidence in thy mercy, that we may take all these thy just punishments with meekness, and so be converted unto thy law.

Then shall we, after we have passed this vale of pilgrimage in thy fear, however the world stormeth, or the devil rageth and roareth against us, die in thy favour.

Which petition, for thy Son Jesus Christ's sake, grant unto us; to whom, with thee and the Holy Spirit, be all honour, praise, and dominion, now and for ever. Amen.

THE END.

C Whittingham 21 Tooks Court Chancery Lane London